THE AUSTRALIAN Women's Weekly

Right now, you can start a fascinating journey to Greece with this book. Your passport is our step-by-step recipes where you cook, taste and learn the secrets of Greek-style home cooking. Freshness of ingredients is all-important, with lemons, garlic, olive oil, herbs and spices adding authentic flavours. It is hearty food, great to share with warmth, friendliness and hospitality as you would in Greece. With a meal, put plenty of bread, olives and wine on the table, then linger over it all, with coffee and sweets later. Sometimes, recipes and names vary between regions, but we give you favourites that are delicious under any name.

Pamela Clark

Food Director

# CONTENTS

# APPETISERS & SOUPS

*mezethes ke soupes*

## taramosalata with artichokes *taramosalata me anginares*

1. Remove crusts from bread, soak bread in cold water 2 minutes. Drain, squeeze water from bread.
2. Blend or process bread, tarama, onion, garlic and juice until well combined and creamy. While motor is operating, gradually add oil in a thin stream; process until well combined.
3. Trim base of artichokes so they sit flat. Remove any tough outer leaves and trim remaining leaves with scissors. Rinse artichokes under cold water. Add to pan of boiling water, boil, uncovered, 30 minutes or until artichoke hearts are tender when pricked with a fork; drain, rinse under cold water.
4. Open artichokes slightly and carefully remove the inner soft leaves and hairy choke with a teaspoon. Serve taramosalata in artichoke hearts, as a dip with artichoke leaves and bread, or as an accompaniment to Greek meals.

**serves 6**

- 4 slices stale white bread
- 100g tarama (salted fish roe)
- ½ small onion, grated
- 1 small clove garlic, crushed
- ¼ cup (60ml) lemon juice
- ⅔ cup (160ml) olive oil
- 6 small fresh globe artichokes

*Gradually pour oil into blender; process until well combined.*

*Trim base of artichokes to sit flat; trim outer leaves.*

*Remove inner soft leaves and hairy choke with a teaspoon.*

CONTENTS 4 LITRES
ΤΡΙΦΥΛΙΑ
ΤΡΙΦΥΛΙΑ
BRAND

# seafood soup *kakavia*

- 300g medium uncooked prawns
- 1 small lobster tail (about 200g)
- 1.2kg fish heads and bones
- 1 large onion, chopped
- 1 trimmed celery stalk, chopped
- 1 medium carrot, chopped
- 2 bay leaves
- 8 sprigs fresh lemon thyme
- 2 litres (8 cups) water
- 2 tablespoons olive oil
- 1 large leek, sliced
- 3 cloves garlic, thinly sliced
- 1 trimmed celery stalk, chopped, extra
- 3 medium tomatoes, peeled, seeded, chopped
- 1½ tablespoons chopped fresh lemon thyme
- ½ cup (125ml) dry white wine
- ¼ cup (60ml) tomato paste
- ½ teaspoon fennel seeds
- 1 large potato, chopped
- 1 teaspoon sugar
- 250g firm white fish fillets
- 150g scallops
- 2 tablespoons chopped fresh parsley
- ¼ cup (60ml) lemon juice

1. Shell and devein prawns, discard heads, reserve shells. Remove lobster meat from shell, reserve shell. Reserve prawn and lobster meat for soup. Combine reserved prawn and lobster shells, fish heads and bones, onion, celery, carrot, bay leaves, lemon thyme sprigs and water in saucepan; simmer, uncovered, 35 minutes. Strain stock, discard fish heads and bones and vegetables. You will need 1.5 litres (6 cups) stock.
2. Heat oil in saucepan, add leek and garlic; cook, stirring, until leek is soft. Add extra celery, tomatoes, chopped lemon thyme and wine; boil, uncovered, until vegetables are soft.
3. Stir in combined stock, paste and seeds; simmer, uncovered, 10 minutes. Add potato, simmer 5 minutes or until potato is just tender. Add sugar; season with salt and pepper to taste.
4. Cut reserved lobster meat and fish into 4cm pieces. Add fish pieces to soup, simmer 1 minute; add lobster and reserved prawns, simmer further minute. Add scallops, bring to boil, stir in parsley and juice.

**serves 6**

*Combine seafood stock ingredients and water in saucepan.*

*Stir in combined stock, paste and fennel seeds; simmer 10 minutes.*

*Add fish pieces to soup, remaining seafood, parsley and juice.*

# cheese turnovers *tiropitakia*

1 Sift flours into bowl, stir in oil and water; mix to a soft dough. Knead dough on lightly floured surface until smooth. Cover, refrigerate 1 hour.
2 Preheat oven to moderately hot. Lightly grease oven trays.
3 Divide dough into quarters. Roll each quarter until 2mm thick. Cut into 8cm rounds with decorative cutter.
4 Combine all filling ingredients in bowl; mix well.
5 Spoon 1½ teaspoons of filling into centre of each pastry round, brush edges with a little water, fold rounds in half, press edges to seal. Place turnovers on prepared trays; brush with combined egg yolk and milk. Bake in moderately hot oven 20 minutes or until lightly browned; cool on trays. Turnovers can be served warm or cold.

**makes about 28**

1½ cups (225g) self-raising flour
1½ cups (225g) plain flour
¾ cup (180ml) olive oil
¾ cup (180ml) warm water
1 egg yolk
2 teaspoons milk

**FILLING**
100g fetta cheese, grated
½ cup (100g) ricotta cheese
1 egg, beaten lightly
pinch ground nutmeg
ground black pepper

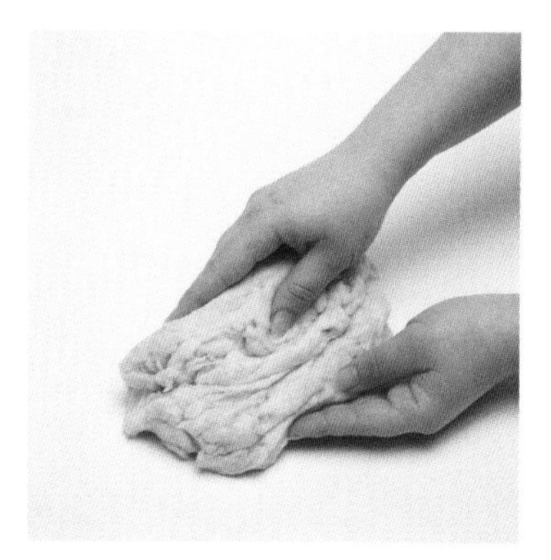

*Knead soft dough on lightly floured surface until smooth.*

*Cut 8cm rounds from dough using a decorative cutter.*

*Spoon filling into centre, brush edges with water; fold and seal.*

# chicken soup with egg and lemon *kotosoupa me avgolemono*

- 1.4kg chicken
- 4 litres (16 cups) water
- 2 black peppercorns
- 1 medium carrot, chopped
- 1 medium onion, chopped
- 1 celery stalk, chopped
- ½ cup (100g) short-grain rice
- 2 eggs
- ¼ cup (60ml) lemon juice

1. Combine chicken, water, peppercorns, carrot, onion and celery in large saucepan; simmer, covered, 2 hours.
2. Remove chicken from pan, reserve for another use. Strain stock through sieve; discard vegetables. Cool stock; cover, refrigerate overnight. Skim fat from stock. You will need 2.25 litres (9 cups) stock.
3. Bring stock to boil in saucepan; add rice, cook, partly covered, 15 minutes or until rice is tender, stirring occasionally. Season with salt and pepper to taste.
4. Just before serving, whisk eggs and juice in medium bowl until frothy. Gradually whisk in 2 cups (500ml) of hot stock. Whisk egg and lemon mixture into pan of remaining hot stock and rice mixture; whisk over heat until heated through. Do not boil.

**serves 6 to 8**

*Combine chicken and remaining stock ingredients in pan; simmer.*

*Add rice to boiling stock; cook 15 minutes or until tender.*

*Gradually whisk hot stock into combined eggs and juice.*

# haricot bean soup *fassoulatha*

2 cups (400g) dried haricot beans
1 tablespoon olive oil
2 medium onions, chopped finely
1 clove garlic, crushed
2 large carrots, chopped finely
2 trimmed celery stalks, chopped finely
1.5kg tomatoes, peeled, seeded, chopped
2 vegetable stock cubes
⅓ cup (80ml) tomato paste
2.5 litres (10 cups) hot water
¼ cup chopped fresh flat-leaf parsley

1 Place beans in bowl, cover well with water; cover, stand overnight. Drain beans, rinse well.
2 Heat oil in saucepan, add onions and garlic; cook, stirring, until soft. Add carrots and celery, cook over low heat, stirring mixture occasionally, 10 minutes. Stir in tomatoes, crumbled stock cubes and paste.
3 Add beans and hot water; simmer, covered, 1½ hours or until beans are tender. Stir in two-thirds of the parsley; season with salt and pepper to taste.
4 Divide soup among serving bowls; serve, sprinkled with remaining parsley.

**serves 8 to 10**

*Soak beans in plenty of water overnight; drain, rinse well.*

*Stir in tomatoes, crumbled stock cubes and tomato paste.*

*Stir two-thirds of the parsley into the soup.*

# prawns with fetta *garithes me feta*

24 large uncooked prawns (about 1.4kg)

2 tablespoons olive oil

4 green onions, chopped

2 teaspoons grated lemon rind

1 teaspoon lemon pepper

1 tablespoon chopped fresh oregano

1 tablespoon chopped fresh parsley

1 tablespoon chopped fresh thyme

2 medium tomatoes, peeled, seeded, chopped

200g fetta cheese, crumbled

**TOMATO SAUCE**

30g butter

1 medium onion, chopped finely

4 cloves garlic, crushed

425g can tomatoes

2 tablespoons tomato paste

⅓ cup (80ml) dry white wine

½ cup (125ml) chicken stock

½ teaspoon sugar

1. Make tomato sauce.
2. Shell prawns, leaving tails intact. Remove dark vein using sharp knife.
3. Heat oil in large frying pan, add prawns, onions, rind and lemon pepper; cook, stirring, until prawns change colour.
4. Stir in the tomato sauce, herbs and tomatoes; stir over heat until heated through. Serve sprinkled with cheese.

**TOMATO SAUCE** Heat butter in saucepan, add onion and garlic; cook, stirring, until onion is soft. Add undrained crushed tomatoes and remaining ingredients; stir until boiling. Blend or process sauce until smooth; strain.

**serves 6**

*Blend or process tomato sauce until smooth; strain.*

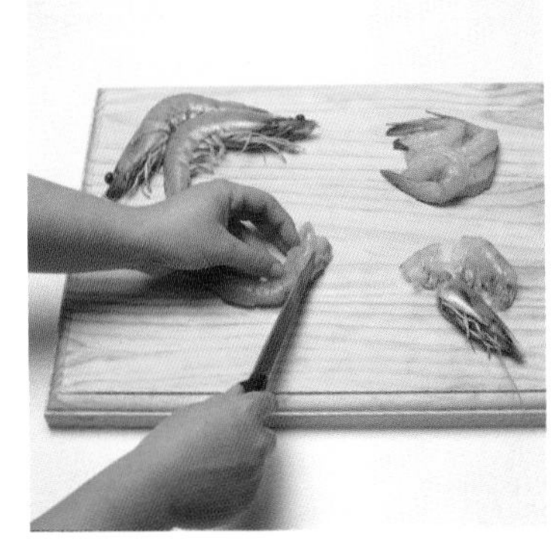

*Shell prawns, leaving tails intact. Remove dark vein using knife.*

*Cook prawns, onions, rind and pepper until prawns change colour.*

# zucchini fritters with yogurt dip *kolokithokeftethes me tzatziki*

1. Combine zucchini, onion, flour, eggs and herbs in bowl; season to taste with salt and pepper.
2. Shallow-fry level ¼ cups (60ml) of mixture in hot oil until lightly browned underneath; flatten slightly. Turn fritters, cook until well browned on other side and cooked through; drain on absorbent paper.
3. Meanwhile, combine all yogurt dip ingredients in bowl; mix well. Serve fritters with yogurt dip.

**makes about 15**

5 large zucchini (750g), grated
1 medium onion, grated
½ cup (75g) plain flour
3 eggs, beaten lightly
1 tablespoon chopped fresh oregano
1 tablespoon chopped fresh basil
1 tablespoon chopped fresh parsley
oil for shallow-frying

**YOGURT DIP**

¾ cup (180ml) plain yogurt
1 small green cucumber, seeded, grated
1 clove garlic, crushed
1 tablespoon chopped fresh mint
2 teaspoons lemon juice

*Combine zucchini, onion, flour, eggs and herbs.*

*Shallow-fry fritter mixture until browned both sides; drain.*

*Place filling in centre of each leaf; roll up firmly, folding in sides.*

*Pour juice, water and oil over single layer of rolls.*

# vine leaves with pine nuts and currants *dolmathakia lathera*

***Vine leaves are available from delicatessens and supermarkets.***

300g packet vine leaves in brine
1 tablespoon lemon juice
¾ cup (180ml) water
1 tablespoon olive oil

**FILLING**
¼ cup (60ml) olive oil
1 medium onion, chopped finely
2 tablespoons pine nuts
½ cup (100g) short-grain rice
2 tablespoons currants
½ cup (125ml) water
2 tablespoons chopped fresh parsley

1 Make filling.
2 Rinse leaves under cold water; drain well. Place leaves vein side up on bench, place 2 level teaspoons of filling on each leaf; roll firmly, folding in sides, to enclose filling.
3 Place rolls in single layer over base of large heavy-based saucepan; add combined juice, water and oil. Place a plate on top of rolls to keep rolls in position during cooking. Simmer, covered, over low heat 1 hour.

**FILLING** Heat oil in saucepan, add onion; cook, stirring, until soft. Add nuts; cook, stirring, until lightly browned. Stir in rice and currants, mix well to coat rice in oil. Add water; simmer, covered, over low heat 10 minutes or until liquid is absorbed. Remove pan from heat; cool. Stir in parsley.

**makes about 24**

*Peel skin from baked eggplant; chop flesh roughly.*

*Process eggplant flesh with remaining ingredients until smooth.*

# eggplant dip *melitzanosalata*

1 Preheat oven to hot.
2 Place whole eggplant on oven tray; bake in hot oven 1 hour or until soft. Remove eggplant from oven; cool slightly. Peel eggplant; chop flesh roughly.
3 Process eggplant flesh with remaining ingredients in food processor until smooth. Refrigerate 3 hours or overnight.

**makes about 1½ cups**

1 large eggplant

1 medium onion, chopped finely

¾ cup (75g) packaged breadcrumbs

2 tablespoons plain yogurt

3 cloves garlic, crushed

½ cup chopped fresh parsley

1 tablespoon cider vinegar

1½ tablespoons lemon juice

½ cup (125ml) olive oil

# mushroom fillo triangles *bourekakia me manitaria*

60g butter

1 large onion, chopped

750g flat mushrooms, chopped

¼ cup (20g) grated parmesan cheese

⅓ cup (25g) stale breadcrumbs

14 sheets fillo pastry

100g butter, melted, extra

1 Heat butter in saucepan; cook onion, stirring, until soft. Add mushrooms; cook, stirring, until mushrooms are tender and liquid evaporated. Remove from heat, stir in cheese and breadcrumbs; season to taste with salt and pepper.
2 Preheat oven to moderately hot. Lightly grease oven trays.
3 To prevent pastry from drying out, cover with baking paper then a damp tea towel until you are ready to use it. Layer two sheets of pastry together, brushing each with a little extra butter. Cut layered sheets into four strips lengthways. Place 1 tablespoon of mushroom mixture at one end of each strip of pastry.
4 Fold one corner end of pastry diagonally across filling to other edge to form a triangle. Continue folding to end of strip, retaining triangular shape. Brush triangles with a little more extra butter. Repeat with remaining pastry, filling and extra butter. Place triangles on prepared trays. Bake in moderately hot oven 15 minutes or until browned.

**makes 28**

*Place 1 tablespoon mushroom mixture at end of each pastry strip.*

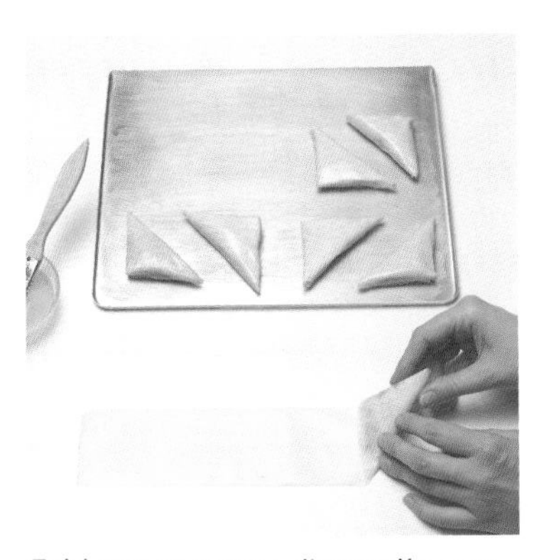

*Fold pastry corner diagonally over filling; continue folding to end.*

## pickled olives *elies se armi*

1 Discard over-blemished olives. Make two cuts lengthways into each olive, through to the stone, using sharp knife.
2 Place olives in sterilised jars (2 litre/8 cup capacity) until jars are two-thirds full. Cover olives with water. Fill a small plastic bag with water, tie bag securely; sit bag on top of olives to keep olives submerged.
3 Scum will appear on surface of water. Change water in jars every day; refill jars with water. Continue changing water for four days for black olives and six days for green olives.
4 Combine salt and the 1 litre (4 cups) of water in saucepan, stir over low heat until salt dissolves; cool. Drain water from jars, pour in enough salted water to cover olives. Pour in enough oil to fill jar completely; seal tightly.

*Pickled olives should be made at least 5 weeks ahead. Store, covered, in a cool, dark place for up to 6 months.*

***Pickled olives are ready to eat after about 5 weeks in salted water. Do not mix black (ripe) and green olives when pickling them.***

1.5kg fresh black or green olives

⅓ cup (75g) fine sea salt

1 litre (4 cups) water

½ cup (125ml) olive oil

*Make two cuts lengthways into each olive, through to the stone.*

*Cover olives with water; sit small plastic bag of water on top.*

*Change water every day; 4 days for black olives, 6 days for green.*

## marinated olives *elies me skordo*

*Pour oil into jar of pickled olives, garlic, lemon and dill.*

1 Combine olives, garlic, lemon and dill in jar (1 litre/4 cup capacity); add oil, seal jar.

*Marinated olives should be made 2 weeks ahead. Store, covered, in a cool, dark place for up to 2 months.*

***It is necessary to pickle olives before marinating them. Marinated olives (right) are ready to eat after about 2 weeks in oil mixture.***

600g drained black or green pickled olives

1 clove garlic, sliced

2 lemon wedges

1 sprig fresh dill

2 cups (500ml) olive oil

# easter soup *mayeritsa*

***Recipe can be made, without egg mixture, a day ahead.***

1 tablespoon olive oil
1kg lamb shanks
3 litres (12 cups) cold water
1 medium onion, quartered
1 teaspoon black peppercorns
2 bay leaves
150g honeycomb tripe
150g lambs' heart
150g lambs' fry
60g butter
6 green onions, chopped
1 clove garlic, crushed
⅓ cup (65g) short-grain rice
2 tablespoons chopped fresh dill
2 tablespoons chopped fresh parsley
3 eggs
⅔ cup (160ml) lemon juice
¼ cup (60ml) water, extra

1. Heat oil in saucepan, add shanks; cook until well browned all over. Remove pan from heat, add water, onion, black peppercorns and bay leaves. Return pan to heat, simmer gently, uncovered, 1½ hours. Strain and reserve stock. You will need 1.75 litres (7 cups) stock. Remove meat from shanks, chop meat into small pieces. Discard bones and onion mixture.
2. Chop tripe, heart and fry into very small pieces. Add tripe to saucepan of boiling water; boil, uncovered, 1 minute. Remove tripe from pan with slotted spoon. Add heart and fry to same pan, boil 1 minute; drain.
3. Heat butter in pan, add green onions, garlic, tripe, heart and fry; cook, stirring, until onions are soft. Remove from pan. Add reserved stock to same pan, bring to boil, add rice; simmer, uncovered, until rice is tender. Stir in onion mixture, lamb, tripe and herbs; season with salt and pepper to taste.
4. Lightly whisk eggs in bowl, gradually whisk in combined juice and extra water. Whisk 1 cup (250ml) hot soup into egg mixture, whisk egg mixture into soup pan; do not boil.

**serves 6 to 8**

*Simmer shanks, water, onion, peppercorns and bay leaves.*

*Cook tripe in boiling water for 1 minute; remove from pan.*

*Whisk 1 cup hot soup into egg mixture; whisk mixture into soup.*

# SALADS & VEGETABLES

*salates ke lahanika*

## rice with leek and silverbeet *spanakorizo*

¼ cup (60ml) olive oil
1 large leek, sliced
2 cloves garlic, crushed
1½ cups (300g) short-grain rice
3 cups (750ml) water
1 bunch silverbeet, washed
2 tablespoons lemon juice
¼ cup chopped fresh parsley

1 Heat oil in saucepan, add leek and garlic; cook, stirring, until leek is soft. Add rice, stir until rice is coated in oil. Add water; simmer, covered with tight-fitting lid, over low heat 15 minutes. Remove pan from heat; stand, covered, 5 minutes.
2 Remove silverbeet leaves from stalks; discard stalks. Slice leaves thinly. Place silverbeet in separate pan; simmer, covered, few minutes or until just limp. Drain.
3 Stir silverbeet, juice and parsley into rice; season with salt and pepper to taste.

**serves 4 to 6**

*Pour water, stirring, into rice and leek mixture.*

*Remove and discard silverbeet stalks; slice leaves thinly.*

*Stir silverbeet into rice, along with juice and parsley.*

# broad beans with peas and artichokes *anginares me koukia*

***You need 1kg fresh peas for this recipe.***

3½ cups (500g) frozen broad beans, thawed

2 tablespoons olive oil

1 large onion, chopped finely

4 cloves garlic, crushed

2 medium carrots, chopped

2¼ cups (350g) shelled peas

425g can tomatoes

20 drained artichoke hearts, quartered

2 tablespoons chopped fresh dill

1 Add broad beans to saucepan of boiling water, boil 1 minute; drain, rinse under cold water until cold, drain well. Peel and discard outer skins.
2 Heat oil in saucepan, add onion, garlic and carrots; cook, stirring, until onion is soft. Stir in peas and undrained crushed tomatoes. Simmer, covered, 10 minutes or until peas are tender.
3 Add beans, artichokes and dill; stir over heat until heated through. Season with salt and pepper to taste.

**serves 4 to 6**

*Peel and discard outer skins from the cooked broad beans.*

*Stir peas and tomatoes into onion and carrot mixture.*

*Add beans, artichokes and dill to pan; stir until heated through.*

# roasted vegetables *briami*

1 Preheat oven to hot. Lightly grease a baking dish.
2 Cut tomatoes into thin slices. Cut potatoes and onions into wedges. Cut zucchini in half lengthways, then into 3cm lengths. Cut celery into 3cm lengths.
3 Add half the tomatoes to prepared dish; top with potatoes, onions, zucchini and celery. Place remaining tomatoes over vegetables.
4 Sprinkle with herbs and garlic; season with salt and pepper to taste, drizzle with oil. Bake, uncovered, in hot oven 30 minutes; stir gently, bake further 40 minutes or until vegetables are tender.

**serves 6**

- 6 medium tomatoes, peeled
- 3 medium potatoes
- 3 medium red onions
- 4 medium zucchini
- 2 trimmed celery stalks
- ⅓ cup chopped fresh parsley
- 1½ tablespoons chopped fresh dill
- 1 teaspoon chopped fresh mint
- 2 cloves garlic, crushed
- ¼ cup (60ml) olive oil

*Cut vegetables into slices, wedges and short lengths.*

*Place remaining tomato slices over chopped vegetables.*

*Sprinkle tomatoes with herbs and garlic; season, drizzle with oil.*

*Simmer onion, lentils, bay leaf, salt and water until lentils are tender.*

*Add onions and celery to lentil mixture; mix well.*

# cold lentil salad *salata faki*

1. Press cloves into onion. Combine onion, lentils, bay leaf, salt and water in saucepan. Simmer, uncovered, 20 minutes or until lentils are just tender; drain, discard onion and bay leaf.
2. Transfer hot lentils to bowl, stir in combined oil, vinegar and oregano; cool. Cover, refrigerate until cold.
3. Stir in onions and celery; mix well. Place lettuce in serving bowl, top with lentil salad.

**serves 4 to 6**

- 2 cloves
- 1 medium onion
- 1 cup (200g) brown lentils
- 1 bay leaf
- 1 teaspoon salt
- 1.25 litres (5 cups) water
- ½ cup (125ml) olive oil
- ⅓ cup (80ml) white wine vinegar
- 2 teaspoons dried oregano leaves
- 2 green onions, chopped
- 2 trimmed celery stalks, chopped finely
- 6 lettuce leaves

# braised vegetables *yachni*

- ¼ cup (60ml) olive oil
- 2 large onions, chopped
- 1 clove garlic, crushed
- 5 medium tomatoes, chopped
- 3 medium potatoes, quartered
- ¾ cup (180ml) tomato puree
- 1 cup (250ml) water
- 250g okra
- 300g green beans
- ½ medium cauliflower, chopped
- 2 tablespoons chopped fresh flat-leaf parsley
- ½ teaspoon sugar

1. Heat oil in saucepan, add onions and garlic; cook, covered, over low heat, stirring occasionally, until onions are very soft.
2. Add tomatoes to pan; simmer, covered, 10 minutes or until soft. Add potatoes, puree, water, okra and beans; simmer, covered, 15 minutes.
3. Add cauliflower, simmer; covered, until potatoes and cauliflower are tender. Stir in parsley, sugar and salt and pepper to taste; stir until hot.

**serves 6**

*Cook onions and garlic in pan until onions are soft.*

*Add cauliflower to saucepan; simmer until tender.*

# greek salad *horiatiki salata*

250g fetta cheese
5 medium tomatoes
2 small green cucumbers
1 large red onion, sliced
1 cup (160g) black olives

**DRESSING**
½ cup (125ml) olive oil
¼ cup (60ml) white vinegar
1 clove garlic, crushed
1 teaspoon sugar
1 teaspoon chopped fresh oregano

1 Combine all dressing ingredients in bowl; mix well.
2 Cut cheese into small cubes, cut tomatoes into wedges, cut cucumber into slices. Combine cheese, tomatoes, onion, cucumbers and olives in bowl; drizzle with dressing.

**serves 6**

*Whisk dressing ingredients in small bowl until well combined.*

*Cut cheese into cubes, tomatoes into wedges; slice cucumbers.*

*Cut whole cauliflower into small florets with sharp knife.*

*Whisk oil, vinegar, juice and herbs in bowl; season to taste.*

# cauliflower with fresh herb vinaigrette *kounoupithi me aromatica*

1 medium cauliflower

¾ cup (180ml) olive oil

¼ cup (60ml) white wine vinegar

1 tablespoon lemon juice

2 tablespoons chopped fresh dill

1 tablespoon chopped fresh parsley

1. Cut cauliflower into small florets. Boil, steam or microwave cauliflower until just tender; rinse under cold water, drain. Transfer cauliflower to large bowl.
2. Combine oil, vinegar, juice and herbs in bowl; season with salt and pepper to taste, mix well. Pour dressing over cauliflower; mix well. Cover, refrigerate until cold.

**serves 4 to 6**

# spring salad *prasini salata*

- 1 medium cos lettuce
- 8 green onions, chopped finely
- 1 tablespoon finely chopped fennel bulb
- 1 tablespoon chopped fresh parsley
- 1 tablespoon chopped fresh dill
- ½ cup (125ml) olive oil
- ¼ cup (60ml) white vinegar
- 1 clove garlic, crushed

1. Finely shred lettuce. Combine onions, fennel, parsley, dill and shredded lettuce in bowl.
2. Add combined oil, vinegar and garlic; season with salt and pepper to taste, mix well.

**serves 4**

*Finely shred the cos lettuce; place in large bowl.*

*Pour combined oil, vinegar, garlic and seasonings over salad.*

# spaghetti with burnt butter sauce *makaronia me voutiro*

1 Add spaghetti to large saucepan of boiling water; cook, uncovered, until just tender; drain.
2 Heat butter in saucepan, cook, stirring, until butter is lightly browned; remove from heat. Stir in garlic; season with salt and pepper to taste. Toss hot pasta with butter mixture and cheese. Sprinkle with extra cheese.

**serves 4**

500g spaghetti

125g butter

2 cloves garlic, crushed

½ cup (50g) grated hard goats' cheese

2 tablespoons grated hard goats' cheese, extra

*Add spaghetti to pan of boiling water; cook until just tender.*

*Remove pan from heat, stir in garlic then pasta and cheese.*

# MAINS

*fayita*

## roast chicken with lemon pistachio rice *kotopoulo yemisto*

1. Make seasoning. Preheat oven to moderate.
2. Place seasoning in chicken, tie legs together, tuck wings under body. Place chicken, breast side up, in large baking dish. Bake in moderate oven 40 minutes.
3. Cut potatoes into 1cm slices. Place potato slices around chicken in dish. Drizzle chicken and potatoes with oil; sprinkle potatoes with thyme and pepper. Bake in moderate oven further 1 hour or until chicken is tender. Remove chicken from dish; keep warm.
4. Increase oven to very hot, bake potatoes further 15 minutes or until potatoes are browned and crisp. Serve roast chicken with potatoes.

**SEASONING** Heat oil in saucepan, add onion; cook, stirring, until soft. Stir in rice until well coated. Stir in stock; simmer, covered, 20 minutes or until rice is tender and liquid has been absorbed. Remove from heat, stir in nuts, thyme and rind; cool.

**serves 4**

1.4kg chicken

4 large potatoes

¼ cup (60ml) olive oil

2 teaspoons chopped fresh thyme

**SEASONING**

¼ cup (60ml) olive oil

1 medium onion, chopped

⅓ cup (65g) long-grain rice

1 cup (250ml) chicken stock

1 cup (150g) pistachios

2 teaspoons chopped fresh thyme

2 teaspoons grated lemon rind

*Stir pistachios, thyme and rind into rice mixture.*

*Spoon seasoning into chicken cavity; tie legs together, tuck wings under.*

*Sprinkle chopped thyme over oiled potato slices.*

# chicken with spinach and fetta *kotopoulo me spanaki ke feta*

¾ bunch (about 500g) spinach

75g fetta cheese, crumbled

4 single chicken breast fillets

1 tablespoon olive oil

⅓ cup (80ml) cream

2 tablespoons chopped fresh parsley

**SAUCE**

60g butter

2 tablespoons plain flour

1 cup (250ml) chicken stock

1 cup (250ml) dry white wine

1. Add washed spinach to saucepan; cook, stirring, until just wilted. Drain well; cool.
2. Combine spinach and cheese in bowl. Cut pocket in side of chicken, fill with spinach mixture; secure with toothpicks.
3. Heat oil in frying pan, add chicken; cook until browned both sides.
4. Make sauce. Pour over chicken; simmer, covered, 25 minutes. Stir in cream and parsley, stir until heated through.

**SAUCE** Melt butter in saucepan, add flour; stir over heat until bubbling. Remove from heat, gradually stir in stock and wine; stir over heat until sauce boils and thickens.

**serves 4**

*Cut pocket in side of chicken, fill with spinach mixture.*

*Remove pan from heat, stir stock and wine into flour mixture.*

*Pour sauce over chicken; simmer, covered, 25 minutes.*

# creamy chicken pie *kotopita*

1. Preheat oven to moderate. Lightly grease 23cm pie dish.
2. Heat butter in frying pan, add bacon, onions and garlic; cook, stirring, until bacon is crisp. Add flour; stir until combined. Remove from heat, gradually stir in milk. Return to heat and stir until mixture boils and thickens; cool. Stir in chicken, cheese and eggs.
3. To prevent pastry from drying out, cover with baking paper then a damp tea towel until ready to use. Layer two sheets of pastry together, brushing each with a little extra butter. Fold layered sheets in half lengthways; place in prepared dish with edges overhanging. Repeat with another six pastry sheets and more extra butter, overlapping strips clockwise around dish until covered.
4. Spoon chicken mixture into dish, fold overhanging edges back onto filling; brush all over with more extra butter.
5. Layer remaining two pastry sheets with more extra butter; fold in half crossways, buttered sides together. Place pastry on top of pie, trim edge. Brush top lightly with more extra butter. Bake in moderate oven 35 minutes or until browned and heated through; cover with foil if pie begins to over-brown.

**serves 6 to 8**

60g butter

4 bacon rashers, chopped

6 green onions, chopped

2 cloves garlic, crushed

2 tablespoons plain flour

1½ cups (375ml) milk

3½ cups (525g) chopped cooked chicken

⅓ cup (25g) grated parmesan cheese

2 eggs, beaten lightly

10 sheets fillo pastry

80g butter, melted, extra

*Layer two sheets of buttered pastry together; fold in half lengthways.*

*Fold overhanging pastry back onto filling; brush with extra butter.*

*Fold remaining sheets of buttered pastry in half; place on pie.*

# chicken with figs in red wine *kotopoulo krasato me sika*

- 8 chicken thigh cutlets
- 2 tablespoons plain flour
- 1½ tablespoons ground coriander
- pinch cayenne pepper
- 1½ teaspoons ground cumin
- ⅓ cup (80ml) olive oil
- 2 medium onions, sliced
- 6 cloves garlic
- 2 bay leaves
- 8 fresh figs
- 1¼ cups (310ml) dry red wine
- 1 teaspoon chicken stock powder
- 2 teaspoons grated lemon rind
- 1 teaspoon lemon juice
- 2 teaspoons cornflour
- 1 tablespoon water
- 2 tablespoons chopped fresh flat-leaf parsley

1. Preheat oven to moderate.
2. Remove skin from chicken. Toss chicken in combined flour and spices, shake away excess flour. Heat oil in frying pan, add chicken in batches, cook until well browned all over; drain on absorbent paper. Add onions and garlic to same pan; cook, covered, over low heat, stirring occasionally, 10 minutes or until onions are very soft.
3. Transfer chicken and onion mixture to large heatproof dish (1.75 litre/7 cup capacity). Add bay leaves, figs and combined wine and stock powder; cook, covered, in moderate oven 1¼ hours or until chicken is very tender.
4. Remove chicken, figs and bay leaves from dish; discard bay leaves. Add rind, juice and blended cornflour and water; stir over heat until mixture boils and thickens.
5. Return chicken and figs to pan, stir until heated through; sprinkle with parsley.

**serves 4**

*Cook onions and garlic until onions are very soft.*

*Pour wine and stock powder over chicken, bay leaves and figs.*

*Remove chicken and figs; stir in blended cornflour until thickened.*

# roast quail in vine leaves *ortikia se klimatofila*

1 Place quail in large bowl, pour over combined rinds, honey, oil, juices, thyme, brandy and salt and pepper to taste. Cover, refrigerate 3 hours or overnight.
2 Preheat oven to moderately hot.
3 Rinse vine leaves under cold water; drain, pat dry with absorbent paper. Remove quail from marinade; reserve marinade. Fold wings under quail; fold vine leaves in half crossways. Wrap two leaves around each quail; secure legs together with toothpicks.
4 Place quail in two baking dishes; bake, uncovered, in moderately hot oven 35 minutes or until tender, basting with reserved marinade every 10 minutes. Serve quail drizzled with pan juices.

serves 6

***Vine leaves are available from delicatessens and supermarkets.***

12 quail
2 tablespoons grated lemon rind
1 tablespoon grated orange rind
½ cup (125ml) honey
⅓ cup (80ml) olive oil
½ cup (125ml) lemon juice
⅓ cup (80ml) orange juice
¼ cup chopped fresh lemon thyme
½ cup (125ml) brandy
24 packaged vine leaves in brine

*Place quail in large bowl; pour over combined marinade ingredients.*

*Wrap two vine leaves around each quail; secure legs with toothpicks.*

*Bake quail, basting with marinade every 10 minutes, until tender.*

# rabbit with apricots and cracked wheat

*kouneli me verikoko ke pligouri*

1⅓ cups (200g) dried apricots
¾ cup (180ml) dry white wine
2kg rabbit pieces
plain flour
⅓ cup (80ml) olive oil
2 large onions, sliced
2 cloves garlic, crushed
1 tablespoon plain flour, extra
2 bay leaves
3 trimmed celery stalks, chopped
2½ cups (625ml) chicken stock
2 teaspoons honey
2 teaspoons chopped fresh thyme
2 teaspoons chopped fresh rosemary
2 teaspoons coriander seeds, crushed
1 tablespoon brown vinegar
2 teaspoons chopped fresh thyme, extra
2 teaspoons chopped fresh rosemary, extra

**CRACKED WHEAT**
2 tablespoons olive oil
2 cups (500ml) water
1 cup (160g) cracked wheat
½ cup (80g) black olives, sliced
2 tablespoons chopped fresh parsley

1. Combine apricots and wine in bowl; cover, stand 1 hour.
2. Preheat oven to moderately hot.
3. Toss rabbit in flour, shake away excess flour. Heat oil in frying pan; cook rabbit, in batches, until browned all over. Transfer rabbit to ovenproof dish (3 litre/12 cup capacity). Add onions and garlic to same frying pan; cook, stirring, until onions are soft. Stir in extra flour, cook until grainy.
4. Gradually stir in bay leaves, celery, stock, undrained apricots, honey, thyme, rosemary, seeds and vinegar. Bring to boil; pour mixture over rabbit, stir well.
5. Bake, covered, in moderately hot oven 2 hours or until rabbit is tender.
6. Meanwhile, make cracked wheat.
7. Stir extra thyme and extra rosemary into rabbit; season with salt and pepper to taste. Serve rabbit with cracked wheat.

**CRACKED WHEAT** Combine oil and water in saucepan, bring to boil, add wheat; simmer, covered, over low heat 15 minutes. Remove from heat, stand, covered, 10 minutes. Add olives and parsley; season with salt and pepper to taste, stir lightly with fork.

**serves 6**

*Pour wine over apricots in small bowl; cover, stand 1 hour.*

*Cook rabbit pieces, in batches, until browned all over.*

*Add apricots to pan containing bay leaves, celery and stock.*

# greek sausages in tomato sauce *souzoukakia*

1 Combine mince, breadcrumbs, onion, garlic, thyme, oregano, cumin and egg in bowl, season with salt and pepper to taste; mix well. Roll 2 level tablespoons of mixture into sausage shape. Repeat with remaining mince mixture.
2 Heat oil in frying pan; cook sausages, in batches, turning, until well browned. Drain on absorbent paper.
3 Make tomato sauce.
4 Add sausages to tomato sauce; simmer, covered, 10 minutes or until cooked through. Sprinkle with mint before serving.

**TOMATO SAUCE** Heat oil in saucepan, add onion and garlic; cook, stirring, until onion is soft. Add wine; simmer, uncovered, until reduced by half. Stir in undrained crushed tomatoes and remaining ingredients, season with salt and pepper to taste; simmer, uncovered, 10 minutes or until sauce is slightly thickened.

**serves 4 to 6**

800g minced beef
1 cup (70g) stale breadcrumbs
1 medium onion, chopped finely
2 cloves garlic, crushed
2 tablespoons chopped fresh thyme
2 tablespoons chopped fresh oregano
½ teaspoon ground cumin
1 egg, beaten lightly
2 tablespoons olive oil
2 tablespoons chopped fresh mint

TOMATO SAUCE
2 tablespoons olive oil
1 medium onion, chopped finely
2 cloves garlic, crushed
½ cup (125ml) dry red wine
2 x 425g cans tomatoes
⅓ cup (80ml) tomato paste
1 cup (250ml) chicken stock
2 tablespoons chopped fresh oregano
2 teaspoons sugar
pinch ground cinnamon

*Roll 2 tablespoons mince mixture into sausage shape.*

*Cook sausages, in batches, until well browned on all sides.*

*Simmer sausages in tomato sauce for 10 minutes; add mint.*

# beef with fennel *kreas me maratho*

- ⅓ cup (80ml) olive oil
- 1 large onion, sliced
- 3 cloves garlic, sliced
- 1.25kg piece beef silverside
- ½ cup (125ml) dry red wine
- 2 cups (500ml) beef stock
- 6 sprigs fresh thyme
- 2 bay leaves
- 3 sprigs fresh oregano
- 1½ small fennel bulbs
- 2 tablespoons pine nuts, toasted
- ¼ cup chopped fresh parsley

1. Heat half the oil in frying pan, add onion and garlic; cook, stirring, until onion is soft; drain on absorbent paper. Sprinkle beef with salt and pepper to taste. Heat remaining oil in same pan, add beef; cook, turning, until browned all over.
2. Return onion mixture to pan, add combined wine and stock and herbs; cook, covered, over low heat 1½ hours, turning beef once during cooking.
3. Cut fennel into wedges, place in pan with beef; cook, covered, over low heat further 30 minutes or until beef and fennel are tender. Remove beef from pan, stand 10 minutes before serving.
4. Serve sliced beef with fennel and strained cooking liquid. Sprinkle with pine nuts and parsley.

**serves 6**

*Cook beef, turning, until browned all over.*

*Pour combined wine and stock into beef and onion.*

*Place fennel in pan with beef; cook until both are tender.*

# pastitso *pastitso*

1 Preheat oven to moderate. Grease shallow ovenproof dish (2.5 litre/10 cup capacity).
2 Make meat sauce.
3 Meanwhile, add pasta to large pan of boiling water, boil, uncovered, until just tender; drain. Combine hot pasta, eggs and cheese in bowl; mix well.
4 Meanwhile, make topping.
5 Press pasta over base of prepared dish.Top pasta evenly with meat sauce, pour over topping, smooth surface; sprinkle with breadcrumbs. Bake, uncovered, in moderate oven 1 hour or until lightly browned. Stand 10 minutes before serving.

**MEAT SAUCE** Heat oil in pan, add onions and mince; cook, stirring, until mince is well browned. Stir in undrained crushed tomatoes, paste, water, wine, stock powder and cinnamon; simmer, uncovered, until thick. Cool. Stir in egg.

**TOPPING** Melt butter in pan, add flour; stir over heat until bubbling, remove from heat, gradually stir in milk. Stir over heat until sauce boils and thickens, stir in cheese; cool slightly. Stir in egg yolks.

**serves 6 to 8**

250g macaroni

2 eggs, beaten lightly

¾ cup (60g) grated parmesan cheese

2 tablespoons stale breadcrumbs

**MEAT SAUCE**

2 tablespoons olive oil

2 medium onions, chopped

750g minced beef

425g can tomatoes

⅓ cup (80ml) tomato paste

½ cup (125ml) water

¼ cup (60ml) dry white wine

1 teaspoon beef stock powder

½ teaspoon ground cinnamon

1 egg, beaten lightly

**TOPPING**

90g butter

½ cup (75g) plain flour

3½ cups (875ml) milk

1 cup (80g) grated parmesan cheese

2 egg yolks

*Simmer meat sauce in pan until thickened; cool.*

*Press cooked macaroni mixture over base of prepared dish.*

*Pour topping over sauce, smooth surface; sprinkle with breadcrumbs.*

ATHENS

# beef with thyme and oregano butter *kreas me thimari ke rigani*

1kg piece rump steak

1 tablespoon olive oil

freshly cracked black peppercorns

**THYME AND OREGANO BUTTER**

100g soft butter

1 tablespoon chopped fresh thyme

1 tablespoon chopped fresh oregano

1 small clove garlic, crushed

2 teaspoons lemon juice

1 Make thyme and oregano butter.
2 Cut steak into six pieces. Brush each steak with oil, sprinkle with pepper and season with salt to taste. Barbecue, pan-fry or grill steaks until cooked as desired. Serve with slices of thyme and oregano butter.

**THYME AND OREGANO BUTTER** Beat all ingredients in small bowl with electric mixer or wooden spoon until well combined. Spoon mixture onto a sheet of greaseproof paper in a rough log shape. Fold one side of the paper over roll, then, with a ruler, push against the butter so that the mixture forms a smooth log. Roll the butter in the greaseproof paper; refrigerate.

**serves 6**

*Spoon butter mixture onto sheet of paper in rough log shape.*

*With a ruler, push against the butter so it forms a smooth log.*

*Barbecue, pan-fry or grill steaks until cooked as desired.*

# zucchini and eggplant little shoes *papoutsakia*

1 Preheat oven to moderate.
2 Cut zucchini and eggplant in half lengthways, scoop out pulp with spoon, leaving thin shells; chop pulp finely.
3 Heat oil in large frying pan, add onion and garlic; cook, stirring, until onion is soft. Add mince; cook, stirring, until well browned. Add chopped pulp, undrained crushed tomatoes, combined paste and stock. Bring to boil, stir in rice; simmer, uncovered, 15 minutes or until rice is tender and mixture is thick. Stir in parsley, season with salt and pepper to taste.
4 Meanwhile, make sauce.
5 Place zucchini and eggplant shells on oven trays, fill with mince mixture. Spoon sauce over mince mixture, sprinkle with cheese. Bake in moderate oven 35 minutes or until vegetables are tender and tops are lightly browned.

**SAUCE** Melt butter in pan, add flour; cook, stirring, until mixture is dry and grainy. Remove from heat, gradually stir in milk; stir over heat until mixture boils and thickens. Cool; stir in egg and nutmeg.

**serves 6**

6 medium zucchini
6 medium lady-finger eggplants
2 tablespoons olive oil
1 medium onion, chopped
2 cloves garlic, crushed
400g minced beef
425g can tomatoes
¼ cup (60ml) tomato paste
1 cup (250ml) beef stock
⅓ cup (65g) short-grain rice
2 tablespoons chopped fresh parsley
½ cup (40g) grated parmesan cheese

**SAUCE**
30g butter
1½ tablespoons plain flour
1 cup (250ml) milk
1 egg, beaten lightly
pinch ground nutmeg

*Scoop out zucchini pulp with spoon, leaving thin shells.*

*Add combined paste and stock to mince and onion mixture.*

*Spoon sauce over mince-filled zucchini halves.*

# squid with rice and tomato *kalamarakia yemista*

8 medium cleaned squid hoods (about 1kg)

¾ cup (180ml) tomato puree

½ cup (125ml) dry white wine

⅓ cup (25g) stale breadcrumbs

1 tablespoon olive oil

**RICE FILLING**

¼ cup (60ml) olive oil

1 medium onion, chopped finely

2 cloves garlic, crushed

¾ cup (150g) short-grain rice

½ bunch (about 325g) spinach, shredded

¼ teaspoon ground nutmeg

⅔ cup (160ml) tomato puree

¾ cup (180ml) water

1 Preheat oven to moderate. Make rice filling.
2 Spoon rice filling evenly into each squid hood. Secure openings with toothpicks. Place squid in single layer in greased ovenproof dish (3 litre/12 cup capacity); pour over combined puree and wine.
3 Bake, uncovered, in moderate oven 15 minutes; turn squid over. Sprinkle with combined breadcrumbs and oil; bake further 15 minutes or until top is lightly browned and squid is tender. Stand 5 minutes; remove toothpicks. Cut squid into rings; serve with cooking liquid.

**RICE FILLING** Heat oil in saucepan, add onion and garlic; cook, stirring, until onion is soft. Add rice and stir until coated with oil. Stir in spinach, nutmeg, puree and water; simmer, uncovered, stirring occasionally, until all liquid is absorbed. Cool.

**serves 8**

*Add rice to onion and garlic, stir until coated with oil.*

*Spoon rice filling evenly into each squid hood; secure with toothpicks.*

*Sprinkle combined breadcrumbs and oil over squid; bake.*

# baked lemon and tomato sardines *sartheles lathoriganes*

1 Preheat oven to moderately hot.
2 Cut heads from sardines and remove entrails. Cut through underside of sardines to backbone; rinse under cold water.
3 Cut backbone through at tail end with scissors without piercing skin. Pull backbone out towards head end to remove. Remove small bones, press sardines flat.
4 Place tomato slices in single layer in two 20cm x 30cm lamington pans. Place sardines, skin side up, over tomatoes, pour over combined oil, rind, juice and garlic; sprinkle with herbs. Bake, uncovered, in moderately hot oven 7 minutes or until cooked through.

**serves 4**

8 large fresh sardines (about 400g)

3 medium tomatoes, sliced

⅓ cup (80ml) olive oil

2 tablespoons grated lemon rind

2½ tablespoons lemon juice

2 cloves garlic, crushed

2 tablespoons chopped fresh parsley

1 tablespoon chopped fresh oregano

*Cut heads from sardines; cut through underside to backbone.*

*Pull out backbone towards head; remove small bones, press flat.*

*Place sardines onto tomato slices; spoon oil mixture over sardines.*

ΖΕΥΣ & ΗΡΑ
ΝΙΚΗ ΦΤΕΡΩΤΗ
Κατερίνη

# baked codfish patties with garlic sauce *kroketes bakaliarou me skorthalia*

500g dried salt cod

4 medium potatoes

1 small onion, grated

1 egg, beaten lightly

2 tablespoons milk

2 tablespoons chopped fresh flat-leaf parsley

½ teaspoon ground black pepper

2 tablespoons olive oil

**GARLIC SAUCE**

10 slices (250g) stale white bread

5 cloves garlic, crushed

¼ cup (60ml) olive oil

2 tablespoons lemon juice

1 tablespoon water

2 tablespoons packaged ground almonds

1. Place cod in bowl, cover well with cold water, cover; stand overnight.
2. Drain cod, place in saucepan, cover with cold water; simmer, uncovered, 15 minutes. Drain, pat dry with absorbent paper. Flake cod finely, remove any skin and bones.
3. Meanwhile, boil, steam or microwave potatoes until tender; mash well.
4. Preheat oven to moderately hot. Lightly grease oven tray.
5. Combine cod, potatoes, onion, egg, milk, parsley and pepper in bowl. With wet hands, roll ⅓ cup mixture into a ball; flatten slightly. Repeat with remaining mixture.
6. Place patties on prepared tray, brush patties with oil; bake in moderately hot oven 10 minutes. Turn patties over, reduce heat to moderate, bake further 20 minutes or until lightly browned.
7. Meanwhile, make garlic sauce. Serve codfish patties with garlic sauce.

**GARLIC SAUCE** Trim crusts from bread. Soak bread in cold water 2 minutes. Drain, squeeze as much water as possible from bread. Combine bread and remaining ingredients with salt and pepper to taste in bowl; mix well.

**makes 12**

*Place cod in bowl, cover with water, cover; stand overnight.*

*With wet hands, shape codfish mixture into a ball; flatten slightly.*

*Combine soaked bread and remaining sauce ingredients.*

# snapper cutlets with tomato herb crust *psari plaki*

1 Preheat oven to moderate.
2 Heat oil in frying pan, add garlic, onions and celery; cook, stirring, until onions are soft. Add tomatoes, cook, stirring, until tomatoes are soft; add parsley, mix well.
3 Place fish in single layer in baking dish, sprinkle with oregano; season with salt and pepper to taste. Top with tomato mixture.
4 Layer lemon slices over tomato mixture, pour over combined wine and juice, sprinkle with breadcrumbs. Bake, uncovered, in moderate oven 30 minutes or until fish is tender.

**serves 4**

¼ cup (60ml) olive oil

1 clove garlic, crushed

2 medium onions, sliced

2 trimmed celery stalks (200g), chopped

3 medium tomatoes, peeled, chopped

¾ cup chopped fresh parsley

4 snapper cutlets

1 teaspoon dried oregano leaves

1 medium lemon, sliced thinly

½ cup (125ml) dry white wine

¼ cup (60ml) lemon juice

¼ cup (15g) stale breadcrumbs

*Stir chopped parsley into onion and tomato mixture.*

*Season snapper cutlets, top with tomato sauce.*

*Sprinkle breadcrumbs over lemon slices; bake 30 minutes.*

Ο ΚΟΣΜΟΣ

# octopus in red wine *oktapothi krasato*

2kg baby octopus
1/3 cup (80ml) olive oil
2 cloves garlic, crushed
500g baby onions, quartered
2 bay leaves
1½ cups (375ml) dry red wine
1 cup (250ml) water
¼ cup (60ml) red wine vinegar
440ml can tomato puree
1 teaspoon chicken stock powder
2 teaspoons dried oregano leaves
2 teaspoons sugar
1 tablespoon chopped fresh parsley

1 Cut heads from octopus just below eyes, discard heads; remove beaks. Wash octopus; cut into quarters.
2 Heat oil in saucepan, add octopus and garlic; cook, stirring, until most of the octopus liquid is evaporated.
3 Add onions, bay leaves, wine, water, vinegar, puree and stock powder. Simmer, uncovered, 1½ hours or until octopus are tender, stirring occasionally. Remove bay leaves, add oregano and sugar, season with salt and pepper to taste; mix well. Sprinkle with parsley just before serving.

**serves 4**

*Cut heads from octopus just below eyes, discard heads; remove beaks.*

*Cook octopus and garlic, stirring, until octopus liquid evaporates.*

*Add onions and bay leaves to pan; pour in wine.*

# veal with eggplant and olives *vithelo me melitzana ke elies*

1. Cut eggplant into 2.5cm pieces, sprinkle with salt; stand 30 minutes. Rinse eggplant under cold water, drain; pat dry with absorbent paper.
2. Heat oil in large saucepan, add eggplant; cook until lightly browned. Remove eggplant from pan.
3. Heat extra oil in same pan, add veal in batches; cook until browned all over. Remove veal from pan.
4. Add onions to same pan; cook, stirring, until soft. Return veal to pan, add spices, garlic and bay leaves; cook, stirring, 1 minute.
5. Add undrained crushed tomatoes, paste, water and wine, stir until combined; simmer, covered, over low heat 1 hour, stirring occasionally. Add eggplant pieces; simmer, covered, 20 minutes or until eggplant and veal are tender. Add juice, olives, parsley and sugar; season with salt and pepper to taste, simmer until heated through.

**serves 4 to 6**

1 large eggplant
coarse cooking salt
¼ cup (60ml) olive oil
1 tablespoon olive oil, extra
1kg diced veal
2 medium onions, chopped
2 teaspoons ground cumin
¼ teaspoon ground allspice
½ teaspoon ground cinnamon
½ teaspoon ground coriander
1 teaspoon paprika
¼ teaspoon cayenne pepper
4 cloves garlic, crushed
2 bay leaves
2 x 425g cans tomatoes
¼ cup (60ml) tomato paste
½ cup (125ml) water
1¾ cups (430ml) dry red wine
¼ cup (60ml) lemon juice
½ cup (90g) pitted black olives, quartered
½ cup (90g) pimiento-stuffed green olives, quartered
2 tablespoons chopped fresh flat-leaf parsley
½ teaspoon sugar

*Sprinkle salt over eggplant pieces; stand 30 minutes.*

*Cook veal, in batches, until browned all over.*

*Add eggplant to veal and tomato mixture; simmer until tender.*

# braised veal with pasta

*pastitsada*

1.7kg boned veal shoulder, rolled, tied
4 cloves garlic, sliced
¼ cup (60ml) olive oil
1 cinnamon stick
2 cloves
1 bay leaf
¼ cup (60ml) red wine vinegar
1 cup (250ml) dry red wine
2 tablespoons olive oil, extra
2 large onions, chopped
2 x 425g cans tomatoes
1 teaspoon sugar
pinch cayenne pepper
250g penne pasta
80g hard goats' cheese, grated

1. Preheat oven to slow.
2. Rub veal with salt and pepper. With a sharp knife, make small incisions in veal; insert a slice of garlic in each incision, using half the garlic.
3. Heat oil in large flameproof dish, add veal; cook until browned all over. Add remaining garlic, cinnamon, cloves, bay leaf, vinegar and wine, bring to boil; cover tightly with foil and lid, bake in slow oven 1 hour, turning once.
4. Heat extra oil in saucepan, add onions; cook, stirring, until soft. Add undrained crushed tomatoes, sugar and cayenne; simmer, uncovered, 20 minutes or until thickened slightly.
5. Increase oven to moderately slow. Add tomato mixture to veal in dish, cover; bake in moderately slow oven 2 hours, turning veal occasionally. Remove veal from dish, keep warm. Skim fat from tomato mixture; discard cinnamon stick, cloves and bay leaf.
6. Cook pasta in pan of boiling water, uncovered, until tender; drain. Meanwhile, simmer tomato mixture 15 minutes or until thickened and reduced by half; season with salt and pepper to taste. You will need about 3½ cups (875ml) tomato sauce for this recipe. Slice veal.
7. Increase oven to moderately hot. Combine pasta, half the tomato sauce and half the cheese in bowl; spread over base of ovenproof dish (2 litre/8 cup capacity). Place veal on top of pasta, pour over remaining tomato sauce; sprinkle with remaining cheese. Bake, covered, in moderately hot oven 30 minutes or until heated through.

**serves 6 to 8**

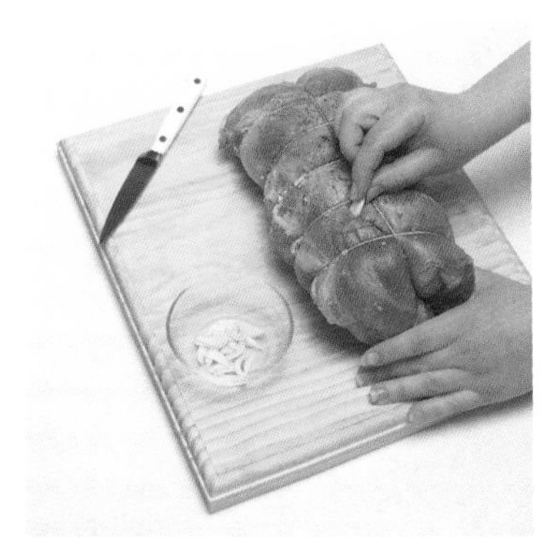

*Insert a slice of garlic in each incision, using half the garlic.*

*Simmer tomato mixture until thickened and reduced by half.*

*Pour remaining sauce over veal and pasta layers.*

# roast pork with oranges and olives *hirino fournou me portokali ke elies*

1. Place pork on bench, skin side up. Run knife 5mm under rind, gradually separating rind from pork. Trim excess fat; discard rind and fat. Roll pork firmly and secure with string at 2cm intervals.
2. Make marinade. Combine pork and marinade in large shallow dish, cover, refrigerate overnight; turn the pork occasionally.
3. Preheat oven to moderately hot.
4. Remove pork from marinade, reserve marinade. Combine oil, honey, ouzo, parsley and garlic in bowl, season with salt and pepper to taste; mix well. Place pork in baking dish. Brush honey mixture over pork. Bake, uncovered, in moderately hot oven 1 hour, brushing occasionally with some of the reserved marinade.
5. Add remaining reserved marinade and olives; bake, uncovered, further 10 minutes or until pork is tender. Remove pork and olives; stir pan juices over heat until slightly thickened. Remove string, serve pork with olives and pan juices.

**MARINADE** Using vegetable peeler, peel rind from oranges and lemons; cut rind into strips. Combine rind strips and remaining ingredients in bowl; mix well.

**serves 6**

2.5kg loin of pork, boned
1 tablespoon olive oil
1 tablespoon honey
1 tablespoon ouzo
1 tablespoon chopped fresh parsley
4 cloves garlic, crushed
1 cup (160g) pitted black olives

**MARINADE**
2 medium oranges
2 medium lemons
¾ cup (180ml) orange juice
¼ cup (60ml) lemon juice
1 tablespoon chopped fresh thyme
2 tablespoons honey
⅓ cup (80ml) ouzo

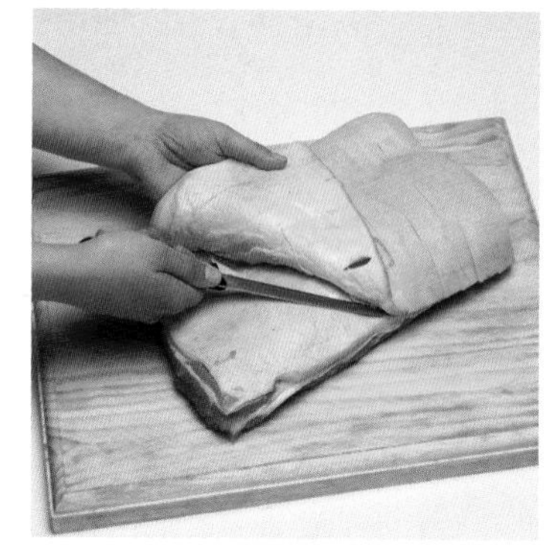
*Run knife 5mm under pork rind, separating rind from pork.*

*Roll pork firmly; secure with string at 2cm intervals.*

*Place pork in baking dish; brush with honey mixture.*

# *hirino me kithonia* pork and quince casserole

- 1 cup (220g) sugar
- 2 cups (500ml) water
- 2 small quince, quartered
- ⅓ cup (80ml) olive oil
- 1 large onion, sliced
- 2 cloves garlic, crushed
- 1kg diced pork
- plain flour
- 1 cup (250ml) dry red wine
- 2 cups (500ml) beef stock
- 1 cinnamon stick
- 2 strips orange rind
- 2 tablespoons chopped fresh thyme

1. Combine sugar and water in saucepan; stir over heat, without boiling, until sugar is dissolved. Add quince; simmer, covered, 5 minutes or until just tender. Cool.
2. Heat half the oil in frying pan, add onion and garlic; cook, stirring, until onion is soft. Drain on absorbent paper.
3. Toss pork in flour, shake away excess flour. Heat remaining oil in same pan; cook pork, in batches, until lightly browned all over. Drain on absorbent paper.
4. Transfer onion mixture and pork to large saucepan, add combined wine, stock, cinnamon, rind and thyme; simmer, covered, 30 minutes, stirring occasionally.
5. Drain and chop quince; discard sugar syrup. Add quince to pork mixture, season with salt and pepper to taste; simmer, covered, further 30 minutes or until pork is tender.

**serves 6**

*Add quince quarters to sugar syrup; simmer until just tender.*

*Cook pork, in batches, until lightly browned all over; drain.*

*Add wine, stock, cinnamon, rind and thyme to pork mixture.*

# pork in garlic and walnut sauce *hirino se saltsa skorthalias*

1 Quarter capsicums, remove seeds and membranes. Grill capsicum pieces, skin side up, until skin blisters and blackens. Peel away skin, cut capsicum into 2cm strips.
2 Heat oil in large saucepan; cook pork, in batches, until well browned. Remove from pan. Add garlic to pan with undrained crushed tomatoes, cinnamon, water and wine; bring to boil. Return pork to pan, add capsicum; simmer, covered, 40 minutes or until pork is tender.
3 Make garlic and walnut sauce.
4 Take a little of the hot sauce from pan; stir into garlic and walnut sauce in bowl. Add garlic and walnut sauce to pan, season with salt and pepper to taste; stir until heated through. Discard cinnamon.

**GARLIC AND WALNUT SAUCE** Cut crust from bread. Soak bread in cold water 2 minutes; drain, squeeze as much water as possible from bread. Process walnuts in food processor until finely chopped; remove to small bowl. Process bread, garlic and vinegar until smooth, add to walnuts in bowl; stir until well combined.

**serves 4**

2 medium red capsicums
2 tablespoons olive oil
4 medium pork loin chops
2 cloves garlic, crushed
410g can tomatoes
1 cinnamon stick
¾ cup (180ml) water
⅓ cup (80ml) dry white wine

**GARLIC AND WALNUT SAUCE**
1 slice white bread
½ cup (60g) chopped walnuts
2 cloves garlic, crushed
¼ cup (60ml) white vinegar

*Cut grilled and peeled capsicums into 2cm strips.*

*Return pork to pan, add capsicum; simmer until pork is tender.*

*Stir a little hot tomato sauce from pan into garlic and walnut sauce.*

# lamb cabbage rolls *dolmathes*

- 12 large cabbage leaves
- 1 tablespoon olive oil
- 1 medium onion, chopped
- 1 clove garlic, crushed
- 500g minced lamb
- ¼ cup (50g) long-grain rice
- 1 small tomato, peeled, chopped
- 1 tablespoon chopped fresh parsley
- 1 teaspoon chopped fresh dill
- pinch ground cinnamon
- 2½ cups (625ml) hot chicken stock
- 20g butter
- 2 teaspoons cornflour
- 2 teaspoons water
- 1 egg, separated
- 2 tablespoons lemon juice

1. Add leaves, in batches, to large saucepan of boiling water, simmer, uncovered, until leaves are soft; drain, pat dry with absorbent paper. Cut any thick core from leaves.
2. Heat oil in saucepan, add onion and garlic; cook, stirring, until onion is soft. Cool. Combine mince, rice, tomato, herbs, cinnamon and onion mixture in bowl, season with salt and pepper to taste; mix well.
3. Divide mince mixture into 12 portions. Place a portion in centre of each cabbage leaf. Fold in sides of leaves and roll up to enclose filling. Place cabbage rolls close together over base of large pan. Pour over stock, dot with butter. Place a plate on top of the rolls to keep them in position during cooking; simmer, covered, over low heat 1 hour or until the rolls are cooked through.
4. Remove rolls from stock; keep warm. Simmer stock, uncovered, until reduced to ½ cup (125ml). Stir in blended cornflour and water; stir over heat until mixture boils and thickens slightly.
5. Beat egg white in small bowl of electric mixer until stiff peaks form; beat in egg yolk. Beat in juice and hot stock mixture. Return sauce to pan, whisk over heat until heated through; do not boil. Serve sauce with cabbage rolls.

**makes 12**

*Simmer cabbage leaves, in batches, in boiling water until soft.*

*Add onion mixture to mince, rice, tomato, herbs and cinnamon.*

*Place portion of mince mixture in centre of leaf; roll up to enclose.*

# lamb in fillo parcels *arni se filo*

1 Heat oil in frying pan, cook lamb quickly, in batches, until well browned all over; drain on absorbent paper.
2 Add extra oil to same pan, add onion; cook, stirring, until onion is soft. Add garlic, undrained crushed tomatoes and herbs; cook, uncovered, 10 minutes, stirring occasionally, or until thick. Cool.
3 Preheat oven to moderate. Grease oven tray.
4 To prevent pastry from drying out, cover with baking paper then a damp tea towel until you are ready to use it. Layer two pastry sheets together, brushing each with some of the butter cut in half crossways. Layer pieces at an angle on top of each other.
5 Place a piece of lamb in centre of pastry, top with quarter of tomato mixture and quarter of cheese; gather edges together to form a parcel, brush with a little more butter. Repeat with remaining pastry, butter, lamb, tomato mixture and cheese. Place parcels on prepared tray. Bake, uncovered, in moderate oven 20 minutes or until browned.

**serves 4**

2 tablespoons olive oil
2 lamb backstraps (about 450g), halved
1 tablespoon olive oil, extra
1 medium onion, chopped finely
2 cloves garlic, crushed
425g can tomatoes
2 teaspoons chopped fresh thyme
2 teaspoons chopped fresh rosemary
8 sheets fillo pastry
80g butter, melted
200g fetta cheese, crumbled

*Cook lamb, in batches, until well browned all over; drain.*

*Layer buttered pastry pieces at an angle on top of each other.*

*Gather pastry edges around lamb, tomato mixture and cheese.*

# eggplant moussaka *moussaka*

2 large eggplants (about 1.2 kg)

coarse cooking salt

¼ cup (60ml) olive oil

2 tablespoons olive oil, extra

1 large onion, chopped

2 cloves garlic, crushed

1kg minced lamb

425g can tomatoes

2 tablespoons tomato paste

½ cup (125ml) dry red wine

2 tablespoons chopped fresh parsley

1 teaspoon sugar

¼ teaspoon ground cinnamon

¼ cup (20g) grated parmesan cheese

½ teaspoon ground nutmeg

**CHEESE SAUCE**

125g butter

⅔ cup (100g) plain flour

1 litre (4 cups) milk

½ cup (40g) grated parmesan cheese

2 eggs

1 Cut eggplants into 5mm slices, sprinkle with salt; stand 20 minutes. Rinse eggplant under cold water; drain, pat dry with absorbent paper. Place eggplant slices in single layer on lightly greased oven trays. Brush with oil, grill on both sides until lightly browned; drain on absorbent paper.
2 Heat extra oil in pan, add onion and garlic; cook, stirring, until onion is soft. Add mince; cook, stirring, until mince is browned. Add undrained crushed tomatoes, paste, wine, parsley, sugar and cinnamon, season with salt and pepper to taste; simmer, covered, 30 minutes.
3 Preheat oven to moderate. Grease ovenproof dish (2.5 litre/ 10 cup capacity).
4 Make cheese sauce.
5 Line prepared dish with one-third of the eggplant, top with half the meat sauce, then half the remaining eggplant, remaining meat sauce and remaining eggplant.
6 Spread cheese sauce over eggplant, sprinkle with cheese and nutmeg. Bake, uncovered, in moderate oven 45 minutes or until lightly browned.

**CHEESE SAUCE** Melt butter in saucepan, stir in flour; continue stirring over heat until bubbling. Remove from heat, gradually stir in milk; stir over heat until mixture boils and thickens. Remove from heat, stir in cheese, cool slightly; stir in eggs, mix until smooth.

**serves 6**

*Brush eggplant slices with oil; grill until lightly browned both sides.*

*Layer eggplant slices and meat sauce; finish with eggplant.*

*Spread cheese sauce over final eggplant layer.*

# roast garlic lamb with lemon potatoes *arni lemonato me patates*

1 Combine oil, rind, juice, wine, pepper and thyme in jug; mix well. Trim excess fat from lamb. Using point of knife, make 12 incisions evenly over top of lamb leg. Place a slice of garlic and some of the rosemary leaves in each incision. Pour oil mixture over lamb; cover, refrigerate 3 hours or overnight, turning lamb occasionally.
2 Preheat oven to moderately hot.
3 Drain lamb, reserve marinade. Place lamb in large baking dish; bake, uncovered, in moderately hot oven 40 minutes.
4 Make lemon potatoes; add to lamb. Bake, turning occasionally, further 50 minutes, or until lamb and potatoes are tender.
5 Remove lamb from baking dish, cover, keep warm. Drain juices from pan; reserve juices.
6 Increase oven to very hot. Return potatoes to oven, bake further 20 minutes or until potatoes are browned and crisp. Heat reserved marinade and reserved juices in pan, bring to boil. Serve with sliced lamb and lemon potatoes.

**LEMON POTATOES** Cut potatoes into 3cm pieces, place in bowl. Pour over combined remaining ingredients and salt; mix well.

**serves 6**

½ cup (125ml) olive oil
2 tablespoons grated lemon rind
2 tablespoons lemon juice
2 tablespoons dry white wine
2 teaspoons seasoned pepper
2 tablespoons chopped fresh thyme
2kg leg of lamb
2 cloves garlic, sliced
1 tablespoon fresh rosemary leaves

**LEMON POTATOES**
12 medium old potatoes
¼ cup (60ml) olive oil
⅓ cup (80ml) lemon juice
1½ tablespoons grated lemon rind
2 tablespoons chopped fresh rosemary
2 tablespoons chopped fresh thyme
1½ teaspoons cracked black peppercorns

*Place a slice of garlic and some rosemary leaves in each incision.*

*Add combined remaining lemon potato ingredients to potato pieces.*

*Add lemon potatoes to lamb in baking dish.*

# garlic and lemon lamb kebabs *souvlakia*

1.5kg lamb leg steaks
3 medium lemons
1 cup (250ml) lemon juice
8 cloves garlic, crushed
¼ cup chopped fresh rosemary
1 tablespoon seasoned pepper
2 tablespoons mild mustard
½ cup (125ml) olive oil
2 tablespoons olive oil, extra
30g butter

1 Cut lamb into 3cm pieces. Using vegetable peeler, peel rind thinly from lemons; cut rind into thin strips. Combine lamb and rind in large bowl, pour over combined juice, garlic, rosemary, pepper, mustard and oil, mix well; cover, refrigerate overnight.
2 Preheat oven to moderate.
3 Drain lamb from marinade; reserve marinade. Thread lamb onto 16 skewers. Heat extra oil in baking dish, add kebabs in batches; cook, turning occasionally, until lightly browned.
4 Return kebabs to baking dish and pour over reserved marinade. Bake, uncovered, in moderate oven 15 minutes or until tender.
5 Remove kebabs from baking dish, boil marinade in dish, uncovered, until reduced to 1½ cups (375ml); add butter, stir until melted. Serve sauce with kebabs.

**makes 16**

*Pour combined marinade ingredients over lamb and rind.*

*Cook kebabs, in batches, in baking dish, until lightly browned.*

*Reduce marinade in dish; stir in butter until melted.*

# fricassee of lamb with lettuce *arni frikase*

1 Heat oil in frying pan, add lamb chops in batches, cook until lightly browned all over; drain on absorbent paper.

2 Add onions, garlic and rind to same pan; cook, stirring, until onions are soft. Return lamb to pan, pour over stock, honey and bay leaves; season with salt and pepper to taste. Simmer, covered, 1¾ hours or until lamb is tender.

3 Add shredded lettuce and herbs; cook, stirring, until lettuce is just wilted.

4 Beat eggs in small bowl with electric mixer until thick; gradually add juice, beat until combined. Add egg mixture to lamb, stir until heated through; do not boil. Remove bay leaves before serving.

**serves 4 to 6**

¼ cup (60ml) olive oil
12 lamb neck chops
3 medium onions, chopped finely
4 cloves garlic, crushed
1 tablespoon grated lemon rind
3 cups (750ml) chicken stock
2 tablespoons honey
3 bay leaves
1 large iceberg lettuce, shredded
¼ cup chopped fresh mint
¼ cup chopped fresh parsley
2 eggs
⅓ cup (80ml) lemon juice

*Cook lamb chops, in batches, until lightly browned all over.*

*Add lettuce and herbs to lamb; cook until lettuce is wilted.*

# goat and haricot bean casserole *katsiki kokkinisto me fasolia*

***You will need to order goat from a specialist Continental butcher; the casserole is equally delicious with lamb.***

2 cups (400g) dried haricot beans
2kg leg of goat, butterflied
¼ cup (60ml) olive oil
2 medium onions, chopped
2 cloves garlic, crushed
2 x 425g cans tomatoes
¼ cup (60ml) tomato paste
½ cup (125ml) dry red wine
1 cinnamon stick
1 tablespoon lemon juice
2 tablespoons chopped fresh parsley

1 Place beans in bowl, cover well with cold water; cover, stand overnight. Drain beans, add to saucepan of boiling water, simmer, uncovered, 30 minutes or until tender; drain well.
2 Cut goat into 3cm pieces. Heat oil in saucepan, cook goat, in batches, until well browned; remove from pan. Add onions and garlic to same pan, cook, stirring, until onions are soft; return goat to pan.
3 Stir in undrained crushed tomatoes, paste, wine and cinnamon; simmer, covered, 2 hours or until goat is tender, stirring occasionally.
4 Add beans, juice and parsley to pan; season with salt and pepper to taste, stir over heat until heated through. Discard cinnamon stick before serving.

**serves 6**

*Add soaked beans to pan of boiling water; simmer until tender.*

*Return cooked goat to pan with onion mixture.*

*Add red wine and cinnamon to goat and bean casserole.*

# TREATS & SWEETS

*zaharoplastiki*

## honey cookies *melomakarona*

1 Preheat oven to moderate. Lightly grease oven trays.
2 Cream butter, rind and sugar in small bowl with electric mixer until combined. Gradually beat in oil until mixture is light and fluffy.
3 Transfer mixture to large bowl, stir in sifted flours, nuts and juice in two batches; mix to a soft dough.
4 Roll level tablespoons of mixture into egg shapes; place on prepared trays, flatten slightly. Mark biscuits lightly with fork. Bake in moderate oven 20 minutes or until browned. Stand biscuits on trays 5 minutes before placing on wire rack to cool.
5 Heat honey in pan until just warm; dip biscuits in honey to coat, place on wire rack over tray. Sprinkle with combined extra nuts and seeds.

**makes about 40**

125g butter
2 teaspoons grated lemon rind
⅓ cup (75g) caster sugar
⅓ cup (80ml) oil
2 cups (300g) plain flour
1 cup (150g) self-raising flour
¼ cup (30g) chopped walnuts
⅔ cup (160ml) orange juice
1 cup (250ml) honey
2 tablespoons chopped walnuts, extra
2 teaspoons sesame seeds

*Gradually beat oil into creamed butter and sugar mixture.*

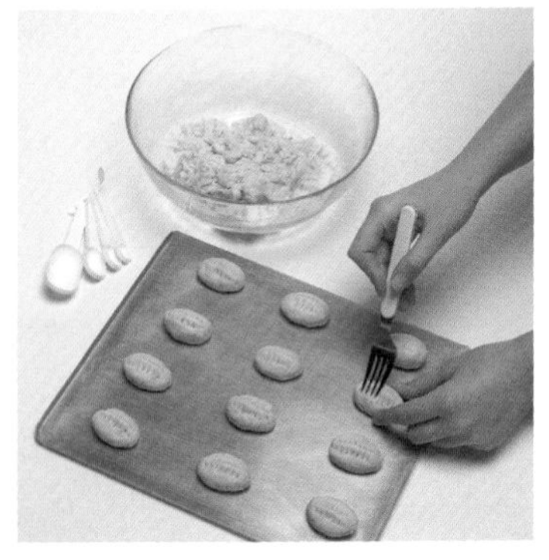

*Place flattened egg-shaped biscuits on trays; mark lightly with fork.*

*Dip biscuits in honey to coat, drain; sprinkle with nuts and seeds.*

# new year cake *vasilopita*

***Part of the Greek New Year tradition is to bake a Vasilopita; the name is derived from St Basil, the patron saint of wishes and blessings, whose feast day is celebrated then. A coin is traditionally placed in the cake, meaning good luck to the recipient.***

250g butter

2 teaspoons grated lemon rind

2½ cups (550g) caster sugar

6 eggs

1 cup (150g) self-raising flour

2 cups (300g) plain flour

½ teaspoon bicarbonate of soda

1 cup (250ml) milk

2 tablespoons lemon juice

¼ cup (35g) pistachios, chopped

¼ cup (35g) walnuts, chopped

¼ cup (40g) blanched almonds, chopped

## TOPPING

¼ cup (35g) pistachios

¼ cup (35g) walnuts, chopped

¼ cup (35g) slivered almonds

¼ cup (55g) sugar

1. Preheat oven to moderate. Lightly grease deep 28cm round cake pan; line base with paper, grease paper.
2. Cream butter and rind in small bowl with electric mixer until light in colour. Add sugar, beat until light and fluffy. Gradually add eggs one at a time, beating well between each addition.
3. Transfer butter mixture to large bowl; stir in sifted flours and soda, and milk in two batches. Stir in juice and nuts.
4. Pour mixture into prepared pan, bake in moderate oven 30 minutes.
5. Meanwhile, combine topping ingredients in bowl; mix well.
6. Remove cake from oven; sprinkle with topping, press on lightly. Bake further 40 minutes. Stand cake 5 minutes in pan; turn out onto wire rack covered with greaseproof paper, turn cake over. Cool.

*Add eggs one at a time to creamed butter, rind and sugar mixture.*

*Stir lemon juice and combined nuts into cake mixture.*

*Sprinkle cake with topping, pressing lightly.*

# easter bread *tsoureki paschalino*

1 Combine yeast, 2 teaspoons of the sugar and milk in small bowl, cover; stand in warm place 10 minutes or until mixture is frothy. Sift flour, salt and spices into large bowl, stir in remaining sugar and combined yeast mixture, butter, eggs and rind; mix to a soft dough.
2 Turn dough onto lightly floured surface, knead 10 minutes or until smooth and elastic.
3 Place dough in lightly oiled bowl, cover; stand in warm place 1 hour or until dough is doubled is size.
4 Meanwhile, make red-dyed eggs. Lightly grease oven tray.
5 Knead dough on lightly floured surface until smooth. Divide dough into three pieces; roll into 60cm strands. Plait strands, place on prepared tray, shape into 24cm ring; pinch ends to seal.
6 Press red-dyed eggs firmly around ring at 6cm intervals. Cover, stand in warm place 40 minutes or until dough is almost doubled in size.
7 Preheat oven to moderately hot. Brush bread with extra egg; sprinkle with chopped nuts. Bake in moderately hot oven 10 minutes. Reduce heat to moderate, bake further 25 minutes or until browned.

**RED-DYED EGGS** Combine dye, vinegar and warm water in jug; stir to dissolve dye. Wash eggs, place in saucepan, cover with cold water. Bring to boil, pour in dye mixture, boil 10 minutes. Remove eggs from pan; cool. Polish eggs with lightly oiled cloth before using.

3 teaspoons (10g) dried yeast
⅓ cup (75g) caster sugar
1 cup (250ml) warm milk
3½ cups (525g) plain flour
1 teaspoon salt
1½ teaspoons ground allspice
½ teaspoon ground cinnamon
90g butter, melted
2 eggs, beaten lightly
2 teaspoons grated lemon rind
1 egg, beaten lightly, extra
1 tablespoon finely chopped blanched almonds

**RED-DYED EGGS**
½ teaspoon Greek red food dye
1 cup (250ml) white vinegar
½ cup (125ml) warm water
4 eggs

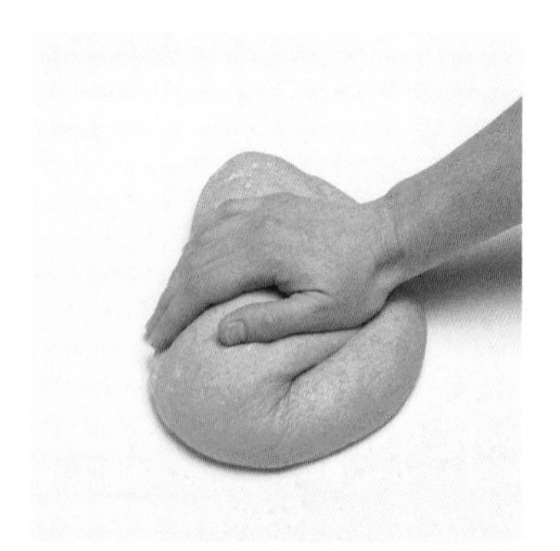

*Knead dough on lightly floured surface until smooth and elastic.*

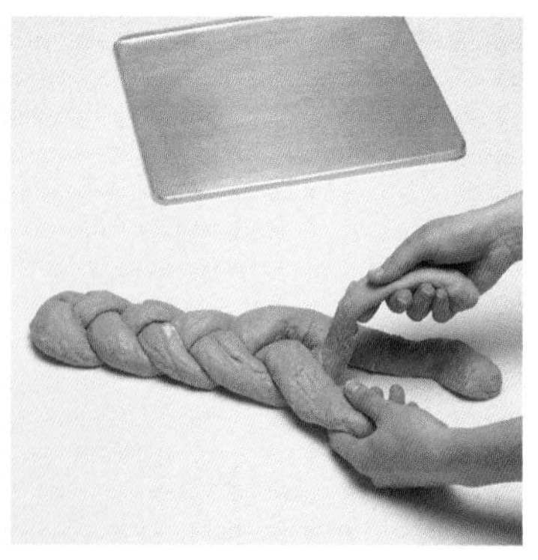

*Plait 60cm strands dough together; place on oven tray, shaped in a ring.*

*Bring eggs to a boil, pour in dye mixture; boil 10 minutes.*

# yogurt cake *yiaourtopita*

125g butter

1 cup (220g) caster sugar

3 eggs, separated

2 cups (300g) self-raising flour

½ teaspoon bicarbonate of soda

¼ cup (25g) finely chopped blanched almonds

1 cup (250ml) plain yogurt

icing sugar

1 Preheat oven to moderate. Lightly grease 20cm x 30cm lamington pan; line base and sides with paper, grease paper.
2 Cream butter and sugar in small bowl with electric mixer until light and fluffy. Add egg yolks one at a time, beating well between additions.
3 Transfer mixture to large bowl, stir in sifted flour and soda in two batches, add nuts and yogurt; stir until smooth.
4 Beat egg whites in small bowl with electric mixer until soft peaks form. Gently fold egg whites into yogurt mixture in two batches. Spread mixture into prepared pan, bake in moderate oven 35 minutes. Turn cake onto wire rack to cool; dust with sifted icing sugar.

*Add egg yolks one at a time to creamed butter and sugar mixture.*

*Stir flour and soda, in batches, into egg and butter mixture.*

*Gently fold egg whites into yogurt mixture in two batches.*

# baklava cigars *poura*

1½ cups (150g) walnuts, chopped finely

½ cup (80g) blanched almonds, chopped finely

¼ cup (55g) caster sugar

1 teaspoon ground cinnamon

½ teaspoon ground cloves

10 sheets fillo pastry

150g unsalted butter, melted

1 tablespoon blanched almonds, chopped finely, extra

¼ teaspoon ground cinnamon, extra

**SYRUP**

1 lemon

1 cup (220g) caster sugar

1 cup (250ml) water

1 cinnamon stick

2 cloves

1 Preheat oven to moderate. Grease oven trays. Combine nuts, sugar and spices in bowl.
2 To prevent pastry from drying out, cover with baking paper then a damp tea towel until you are ready to use it. Cut one sheet of pastry crossways into three even strips; brush each strip with butter. Spoon 3 level teaspoons of nut mixture into a pile on one end of each strip, leaving a 3.5cm border. Fold in sides, brush with butter, roll up tightly to form a cigar shape. Repeat with remaining pastry, butter and nut mixture. Place cigars on prepared trays, brush with remaining butter, bake in moderate oven 12 minutes or until lightly browned; cool on trays.
3 Meanwhile, make syrup. Place cigars in single layer in shallow pan, pour over warm syrup; cool to room temperature. Sprinkle with extra nuts and extra cinnamon.

**SYRUP** Using vegetable peeler, peel rind thinly from half the lemon. Combine sugar and water in saucepan; stir over heat, without boiling, until sugar is dissolved. Add rind, cinnamon and cloves to pan; simmer, uncovered, without stirring, 2 minutes. Cool slightly.

**makes 30**

*Spoon nut mixture on one end of pastry; fold in sides, roll up tightly.*

*Add lemon rind to sugar syrup; simmer 2 minutes.*

*Pour warm syrup over cigars; cool to room temperature.*

# semolina cake *revani*

4 eggs, separated
⅓ cup (75g) caster sugar
½ teaspoon vanilla essence
1 teaspoon grated orange rind
1½ tablespoons ouzo
⅓ cup (80ml) fresh orange juice
½ cup (80g) semolina
⅓ cup (55g) blanched almonds, chopped

**SYRUP**
1 lemon
1 cup (220g) caster sugar
1 cup (250ml) water
1 teaspoon lemon juice

1. Beat egg yolks, sugar, essence and rind in small bowl with electric mixer until light and fluffy. Gradually add ouzo, beat until just combined.
2. Transfer mixture to large bowl, stir in orange juice, semolina and nuts; cover, stand for 30 minutes.
3. Preheat oven to moderately hot. Lightly grease 23cm square slab cake pan.
4. Beat egg whites in small bowl with electric mixer until firm peaks form; fold gently into cake mixture in two batches. Pour mixture into prepared pan, bake in moderately hot oven 20 minutes.
5. Meanwhile, make syrup. Pour warm syrup over warm cake in pan; cool. Cut cold cake into squares to serve.

**SYRUP** Using vegetable peeler, peel rind thinly from lemon; cut rind into thin strips. Combine sugar, water, juice and rind in saucepan, stir over heat, without boiling, until sugar is dissolved; simmer, uncovered, without stirring, 5 minutes. Cool slightly before using.

*Gradually add ouzo to egg and sugar mixture; beat until combined.*

*Gently fold egg whites into cake mixture in two batches.*

*Pour warm syrup over warm cake in pan; cool before serving.*

# honey walnut puffs *loukoumathes*

1. Combine yeast, milk, sugar, egg and butter in large bowl; mix well. Gradually stir in sifted flour; beat until smooth.
2. Stand, covered, in a warm place 1½ hours or until batter doubles in size and bubbles appears on the surface. Beat batter until smooth.
3. Deep-fry level tablespoons of batter in hot oil, turning puffs to give an even colour; drain on absorbent paper.
4. Heat honey in pan until just warm. Place puffs on serving plate, drizzle with honey, sprinkle with cinnamon and nuts.

**makes about 26**

2 teaspoons (7g) dried yeast
1 cup (250ml) warm milk
2 tablespoons caster sugar
1 egg, beaten lightly
60g butter, melted
2 cups (300g) plain flour
oil for deep-frying
⅔ cup (160ml) honey
¼ teaspoon ground cinnamon
¼ cup (30g) chopped walnuts

*Stand batter until it doubles and bubbles appear on the surface.*

*Deep-fry tablespoons of batter in hot oil; drain on absorbent paper.*

*Drizzle warmed honey over puffs; sprinkle with cinnamon and nuts.*

# *glyko portokali* glace orange peel rolls

***A visitor to a Greek home is traditionally made welcome with a spoon sweet or preserve, such as orange peel rolls. Spoon sweets are served to each person with a glass of water. Usually, coffee and a small glass of cognac or liqueur will follow.***

6 large thick-skinned oranges
1.32kg (6 cups) sugar
1.5 litres (6 cups) water
2 tablespoons lemon juice

1. Grate oranges lightly. Cut peel lengthways into six segments; remove peel. Reserve orange flesh for another use.
2. Roll each segment tightly. Push a needle and strong thread through each roll until 12 rolls are threaded; tie ends together securely. Repeat rolling and threading with remaining peel.
3. Place in saucepan of cold water; bring to boil, drain immediately. Repeat boiling and draining process twice more. Cover rolls again with cold water in pan, bring to boil; simmer, uncovered, 40 minutes or until tender; drain. Place rolls on wire rack to dry.
4. Combine sugar and the 1.5 litres of water in large saucepan, stir over heat, without boiling, until sugar is dissolved; stir in juice. Simmer, uncovered, 5 minutes. Add orange rolls, simmer, uncovered, 10 minutes; cool.
5. Bring rolls to boil; simmer, uncovered, 50 minutes or until syrup is thickened slightly. Remove thread from rolls. Place rolls in hot sterilised jars; pour over strained syrup and seal while hot.

**makes about 1.75 litres (7 cups)**

*Recipe can be stored in a cool, dark place for 2 months.*

*Cut orange peel into six segments; remove peel.*

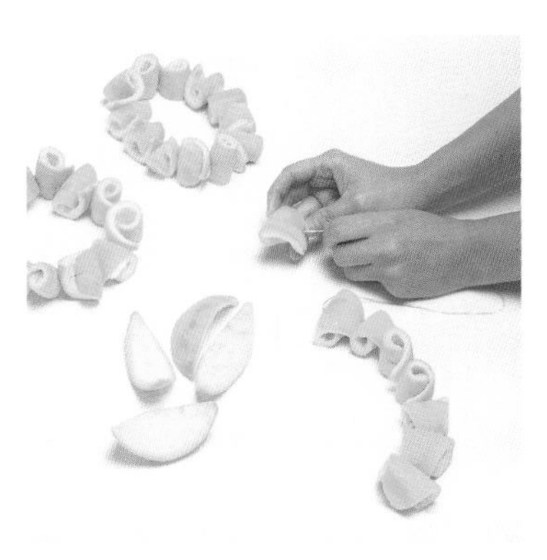

*Roll peel tightly and thread 12 rolls together with a needle; tie ends.*

*Add orange rolls to sugar syrup; simmer 10 minutes.*

# rice pudding *rizogalo*

1. Combine milk, sugar and rind in saucepan, stirring constantly over heat, without boiling, until sugar is dissolved.
2. Bring to boil, add rice; simmer, uncovered, 30 minutes or until rice is tender, stirring occasionally.
3. Remove rind, stir in blended custard powder and extra milk; stir over heat until mixture boils and thickens. Pour mixture into four serving dishes, sprinkle with cinnamon. Serve warm or cold.

**serves 4**

1 litre (4 cups) milk
⅓ cup (75g) caster sugar
5cm piece orange rind
½ cup (100g) short-grain rice
1 tablespoon custard powder
¼ cup (60ml) milk, extra
ground cinnamon

*Combine milk, sugar and rind in pan; stir until sugar dissolves.*

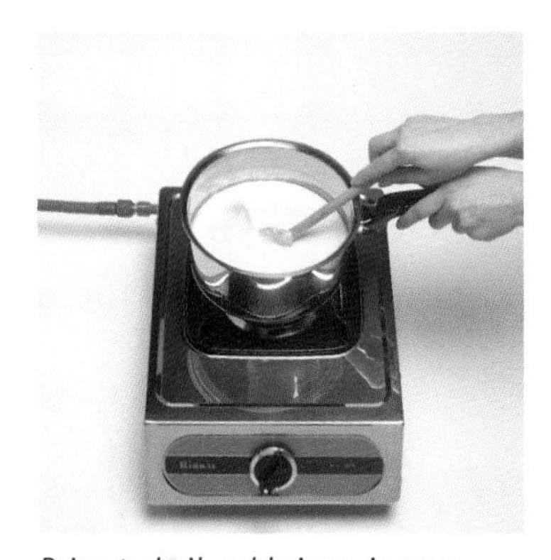

*Bring to boil, add rice; simmer 30 minutes or until rice is tender.*

*Stir in blended custard powder and milk until it boils and thickens.*

# almond pears *amigthalota*

- 3 cups (480g) blanched almonds
- ¾ cup (165g) caster sugar
- ½ cup (80g) semolina, approximately
- 3 egg whites, beaten
- 2 tablespoons orange flower water
- 35 cloves, approximately
- icing sugar, for dusting

1. Preheat oven to moderate. Lightly grease oven trays.
2. Process nuts until fine, transfer nuts to bowl; stir in sugar, semolina, egg whites and orange flower water, mix to a smooth, stiff paste. Add a little extra semolina if the paste is too sticky.
3. Shape level tablespoons of almond mixture into pear shapes; insert a clove in top of each pear. Place on prepared trays, bake in moderate oven 12 minutes or until lightly coloured.
4. Transfer almond pears to shallow tray covered with greaseproof paper; dust heavily with sifted icing sugar while warm.

**makes about 35**

*Mix nuts, sugar, semolina, whites and flower water to a stiff paste.*

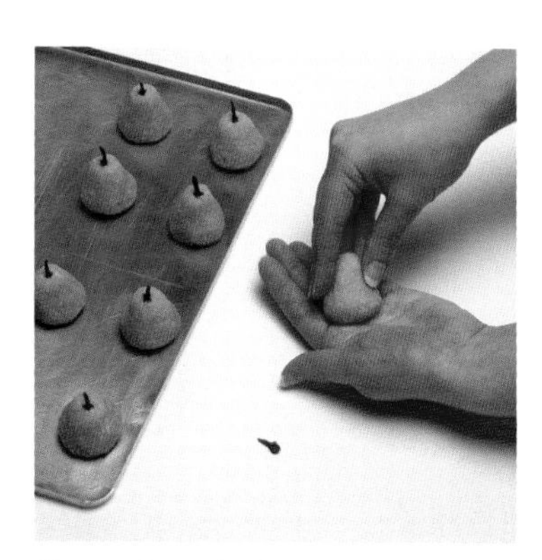

*Shape almond mixture into pear shapes; insert clove in top.*

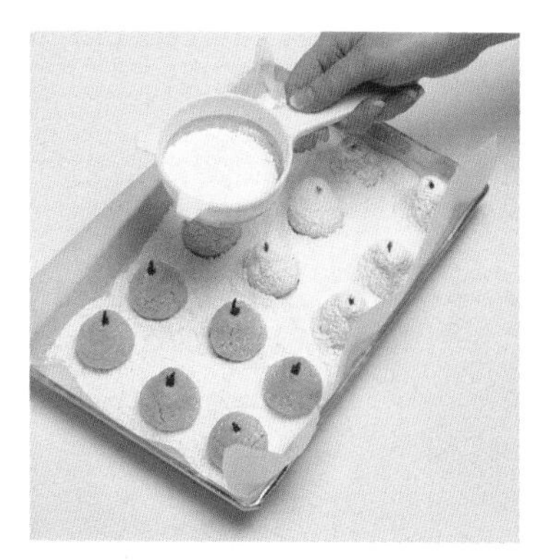

*Heavily dust sifted icing sugar over pears while still warm.*

# custard slice *galaktoboureko*

1 Combine semolina, sugar, cornflour, eggs and rind in bowl; whisk until thick and combined. Bring milk to boil in pan; gradually whisk hot milk into egg mixture. Return mixture to pan.
2 Stir over heat until mixture begins to thicken, gradually add extra semolina; stir until thick, do not boil. Cool slightly.
3 Preheat oven to moderate. Lightly grease 22cm x 30cm ovenproof dish (2.5 litre/10 cup capacity).
4 To prevent pastry from drying out, cover with baking paper then a damp tea towel until you are ready to use it. Brush a pastry sheet with ghee, place into prepared dish so that edges overhang sides. Repeat with five more pastry sheets and ghee, allowing pastry to overhang opposite sides of dish.
5 Pour custard mixture evenly into pastry case. Layer remaining sheets of pastry with ghee, place on top of custard, trim overlapping edges of pastry, fold ends inside dish to enclose filling. Brush with remaining ghee. Using sharp knife, score pastry diagonally, cutting though only one layer of pastry. Bake in moderate oven 45 minutes or until custard is set.
6 Meanwhile, make syrup. Pour cold syrup evenly over hot slice; cool in dish before cutting.

**SYRUP** Using a vegetable peeler, peel rind thinly from half the lemon. Combine sugar and water in saucepan; stir over heat, without boiling, until sugar is dissolved. Add rind and cinnamon; simmer, uncovered, without stirring, 2 minutes. Cool, discard rind and cinnamon.

**serves 8 to 10**

¼ cup (40g) semolina
1½ cups (330g) caster sugar
¼ cup (35g) cornflour
6 eggs, beaten lightly
1 teaspoon grated lemon rind
1 litre (4 cups) milk
½ cup (80g) semolina, extra
12 sheets fillo pastry
125g ghee, melted

**SYRUP**
1 medium lemon
1½ cups (330g) caster sugar
¾ cup (180ml) water
1 cinnamon stick

*Whisk hot milk into egg mixture; return mixture to pan.*

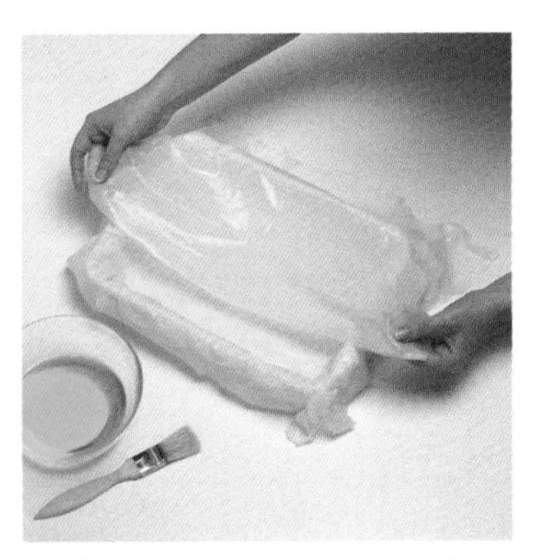
*Brush pastry sheets with ghee; layer in dish with edges overhanging.*

*Score pastry diagonally, cutting through one layer of pastry.*

# glossary

**ALCOHOL** is optional, but gives a particular flavour. Use fruit juice or water instead to make up the liquid content required.

**ALLSPICE** pimento.

**ALMONDS**

**blanched** nuts with skin removed.

**ground** we used packaged commercially ground nuts.

**slivered** nuts cut lengthways.

**AMARETTO** an almond-flavoured liqueur.

**BACON RASHERS** bacon slices.

**BAKING POWDER** a raising agent consisting of a starch, but mostly cream of tartar and bicarbonate of soda in proportions of 1 level teaspoon of cream of tartar to ½ level teaspoon of bicarbonate of soda – this amount is equivalent to 2 teaspoons of baking powder.

**BEANS**

**haricot** small, white, oval beans with a smooth texture and bland in flavour. Require soaking.

**BEEF**

**chuck** from neck area.

**minced** ground.

**round steak** boneless piece of meat from the upper back leg.

**rump steak** boneless piece of meat that covers the hip bone.

**silverside** is cut from the outside portion of the upper leg and cured.

**BEETROOT** round beet.

**BICARBONATE OF SODA** baking soda.

**BREADCRUMBS**

**packaged** use fine packaged breadcrumbs.

**stale** 1- or 2-day-old bread made into crumbs by grating, blending or processing.

**BUTTER** use salted or unsalted (also called sweet) butter; 125g is equal to 1 stick.

**CAPSICUM** bell pepper.

**CHEESE**

**fetta** soft Greek cheese with a sharp, salty taste.

**haloumi** a firm, cream-coloured sheep's milk cheese. A little like fetta in flavour.

**hard goats'** is made from goats' milk; has a pronounced earthy taste.

**parmesan** sharp-tasting hard cheese used as a flavour accent. We prefer to use fresh parmesan cheese, although it is available already finely grated.

**ricotta** is a fresh, unripened light curd cheese.

**tasty cheddar** matured cheddar; use a hard, good-tasting variety.

**CHICKEN** size determined by a numbering system; for example, No 13 is a 1.3kg bird; No 10 is 1 kg. This system applies to most poultry.

**breast fillets** skinless and boneless.

**thigh cutlets** have skin and one bone; sometimes called chicken chops.

**CHICKPEAS** also known as ceci and garbanzos; ½ cup (100g) dried chickpeas equals a 300g can of chickpeas. Soak dried chickpeas overnight in cold water, drain. Add to saucepan of water, bring to boil, simmer, covered, 1 hour or until tender.

**CORIANDER** also known as cilantro and Chinese parsley; its seeds are the main ingredient of curry powder. A strongly flavoured herb, use it sparingly until you get used to the unique flavour. Available fresh, ground and in seed form. Coriander roots and stems can also used.

**CORNFLOUR** also known as cornstarch.

**COUSCOUS** a fine cereal made from semolina.

**CRACKED WHEAT** also called burghul; is wheat which has been cracked by boiling, then dried. It is most often used in Middle Eastern cooking.

**CREAM** fresh pouring cream; has a minimum fat content of 35%.

**CURRANTS** small dried seedless grapes.

**CUSTARD POWDER** pudding mix.

**EGGPLANT** also called aubergine. Ranges in size from tiny to very large, and in colour from pale green to deep purple; eggplant has an equally wide variety of flavours.

**ESSENCE** extract. We used imitation vanilla essence.

**FENNEL** has a slight aniseed taste when fresh, ground or in seed form. Fennel seeds are a component of curry powder. The bulb is eaten uncooked (often sliced) in salads and can also be braised, steamed or stir-fried in savoury dishes.

**FILLO PASTRY** also known as phyllo dough; comes in tissue-thin pastry sheets bought chilled or frozen.

**FLOUR**

**plain** unbleached all-purpose flour.

**self-raising** substitute plain (all-purpose) flour and baking powder in the proportions of 1 cup (150g) plain flour to 2 level teaspoons baking powder. Sift together several times before using.

**GARAM MASALA** a combination of powdered spices, consisting of cardamom, cinnamon, cloves, coriander, cumin and nutmeg in varying proportions. Sometimes pepper is used to make a hot variation.

**GHEE** a pure butter fat available in cans; can heat to high temperatures without burning because of the lack of salts and milk solids.

**GLOBE ARTICHOKES** large flower head of a plant of the thistle.

**GREEN ONIONS** also called scallions, eschalots and green shallots. Do not confuse with the small golden shallots.

**HERBS** we have specified when to use fresh or dried herbs. Use dried (not ground) herbs in the proportions of 1:4 for fresh herbs, for example 1 teaspoon dried herbs instead of 4 teaspoons (1 tablespoon) chopped fresh herbs.

**LAMB**

**backstrap** the larger fillet from a row of loin chops or cutlets.

**fry** lamb's liver.

**minced** ground.

**shank** forequarter leg.

**LENTILS** dried pulses. Many different varieties are available, usually identified and named after their colour.

**LETTUCE**

**cos** also known as romaine; has crisp, elongated leaves.

**iceberg** is a heavy, firm, round lettuce with tightly packed leaves and crisp texture.

**OIL**

**extra virgin** and virgin are the highest quality olive oils, obtained from the first pressings.

**light olive** mild-tasting, light in flavour, colour and aroma, but not low in kilojoules.

**olive** a blend of refined and virgin olive oils, especially good for everyday cooking.

**vegetable** we used a polyunsaturated vegetable oil.

**OKRA** a green, ridged, immature seed pod, also called lady's fingers.

**ORANGE FLOWER WATER** concentrated flavouring from orange blossoms.

**OUZO** aniseed-flavoured Greek spirit.

**PAPRIKA** ground dried capsicum; sweet or hot.

**PARSLEY, FLAT-LEAF** also known as Italian or continental parsley.

**PINE NUTS** small, cream-coloured soft kernels.

**PISTACHIOS** small oval nuts with a green kernel.

**PORK**

**diced** chopped pork.

**loin** from pork middle.

**PRAWNS** shrimp.

**QUAIL** small game birds about 250g to 300g.

**QUINCE** yellow-skinned fruit with hard texture and acid taste.

**RABBIT PIECES** jointed rabbit.

**RICE**

**white** is hulled and polished, can be short- or long-grained.

**RIND** zest.

**SALT COD** dried salted cod; also called baccala.

**SARDINES** small silvery fish with soft, oily flesh.

**SCALLOPS** we used the scallops with coral (roe) attached.

**SEMOLINA** a hard part of the wheat which is sifted out; used mainly for making pasta.

**SESAME SEEDS** there are two types available, black and white.

**to toast** spread seeds evenly onto oven tray, toast in moderate oven for 5 minutes or stir in heavy-based pan over heat until golden brown.

**SILVERBEET** also known as swiss chard. Remove coarse white stems; cook green leafy parts as required by recipes.

**SKEWERS** use metal or bamboo skewers. Rub oil onto metal skewers to stop meat sticking. Soak bamboo skewers in water for at least 1 hour or overnight to prevent scorching or splintering.

**SNAPPER CUTLET** crossways slice of fish with bones.

**SQUID HOODS** convenient cleaned squid (calamari).

**STAR ANISE** the dried star-shaped fruit of an evergreen tree, it has an aniseed flavour.

**STOCK** 1 cup (250ml) stock is the equivalent of 1 cup (250ml) water plus 1 crumbled stock cube (or 1 teaspoon powder).

**SUGAR** we used coarse granulated table sugar, also known as crystal sugar, unless otherwise specified.

**caster** also known as superfine; is fine granulated table sugar.

**icing** also known as confectioners' sugar. We used icing sugar mixture (which contains a small amount of cornflour), not pure icing sugar.

**TARAMA** salted fish roe.

**TOMATO**

**canned** whole peeled tomatoes canned in natural juices.

**paste** a concentrated tomato puree used to flavour soups, sauces, stews and casseroles etc.

**puree** canned pureed tomatoes (not tomato paste). Substitute with fresh, peeled, pureed tomatoes, if preferred.

**TRIPE** honeycomb tripe comes from the stomach of an ox. Tripe is sold cleaned, washed and blanched.

**VEAL**

**diced** chopped veal.

**VERMICELLI** thin, clear rice noodles.

**VINE LEAVES** we used vine leaves in brine; they are available in jars and packets.

**VINEGAR**

**brown malt** made from fermented malt and beech shavings.

**cider** vinegar made from fermented apples.

**white** made from spirit of cane sugar.

**white wine** is based on white wine.

**WINE** we used good-quality dry white and red wines.

**YEAST** allow 2 teaspoons (7g) dried yeast to each 15g compressed yeast if substituting one for the other.

**YOGURT** unflavoured, plain yogurt is used as a meat tenderiser, enricher, thickener and also as a dessert ingredient.

**ZUCCHINI** courgette.

# index

# facts & figures

Wherever you live, you'll be able to use our recipes with the help of these easy-to-follow conversions. While these conversions are approximate only, the difference between an exact and the approximate conversion of various liquid and dry measures is minimal and will not affect your cooking results.

## LIQUID MEASURES

| METRIC | IMPERIAL |
|---|---|
| 30ml | 1 fluid oz |
| 60ml | 2 fluid oz |
| 100ml | 3 fluid oz |
| 125ml | 4 fluid oz |
| 150ml | 5 fluid oz (¼ pint/1 gill) |
| 190ml | 6 fluid oz |
| 250ml | 8 fluid oz |
| 300ml | 10 fluid oz (½ pint) |
| 500ml | 16 fluid oz |
| 600ml | 20 fluid oz (1 pint) |
| 1000ml (1 litre) | 1¾ pints |

## MEASURING EQUIPMENT

The difference between one country's measuring cups and another's is, at most, within a 2 or 3 teaspoon variance. (For the record, one Australian metric measuring cup holds approximately 250ml.) The most accurate way of measuring dry ingredients is to weigh them. When measuring liquids, use a clear glass or plastic jug with the metric markings. (One Australian metric tablespoon holds 20ml; one Australian metric teaspoon holds 5ml.)

## DRY MEASURES

| METRIC | IMPERIAL |
|---|---|
| 15g | ½oz |
| 30g | 1oz |
| 60g | 2oz |
| 90g | 3oz |
| 125g | 4oz (¼lb) |
| 155g | 5oz |
| 185g | 6oz |
| 220g | 7oz |
| 250g | 8oz (½lb) |
| 280g | 9oz |
| 315g | 10oz |
| 345g | 11oz |
| 375g | 12oz (¾lb) |
| 410g | 13oz |
| 440g | 14oz |
| 470g | 15oz |
| 500g | 16oz (1lb) |
| 750g | 24oz (1½lb) |
| 1kg | 32oz (2lb) |

## HELPFUL MEASURES

| METRIC | IMPERIAL |
|---|---|
| 3mm | ⅛in |
| 6mm | ¼in |
| 1cm | ½in |
| 2cm | ¾in |
| 2.5cm | 1in |
| 5cm | 2in |
| 6cm | 2½in |
| 8cm | 3in |
| 10cm | 4in |
| 13cm | 5in |
| 15cm | 6in |
| 18cm | 7in |
| 20cm | 8in |
| 23cm | 9in |
| 25cm | 10in |
| 28cm | 11in |
| 30cm | 12in (1ft) |

## HOW TO MEASURE

When using graduated metric measuring cups, shake dry ingredients loosely into the appropriate cup. Do not tap the cup on a bench or tightly pack the ingredients unless directed to do so. Level top of measuring cups and measuring spoons with a knife. When measuring liquids, place a clear glass or plastic jug with metric markings on a flat surface to check accuracy at eye level.

Note: North America, NZ and the UK use 15ml tablespoons. All cup and spoon measurements are level.

We use large eggs having an average weight of 60g.

## OVEN TEMPERATURES

*These oven temperatures are only a guide. Always check the manufacturer's manual.*

| | °C (CELSIUS) | °F (FAHRENHEIT) | GAS MARK |
|---|---|---|---|
| Very slow | 120 | 250 | ½ |
| Slow | 140-150 | 275-300 | 1-2 |
| Moderately slow | 170 | 325 | 3 |
| Moderate | 180-190 | 350-375 | 4-5 |
| Moderately hot | 200 | 400 | 6 |
| Hot | 220-230 | 425-450 | 7-8 |
| Very hot | 240 | 475 | 9 |

# ARE YOU MISSING SOME OF THE WORLD'S FAVOURITE COOKBOOKS?

*The Australian Women's Weekly* Cookbooks are available from bookshops, cookshops, supermarkets and other stores all over the world. You can also buy direct from the publisher, using the order form below.

| TITLE | RRP | QTY |
|---|---|---|
| Almost Vegetarian | £5.99 | |
| Asian Meals in Minutes | £5.99 | |
| Babies & Toddlers Good Food | £5.99 | |
| Barbecue Meals In Minutes | £5.99 | |
| Basic Cooking Class | £5.99 | |
| Beginners Cooking Class | £5.99 | |
| Beginners Simple Meals | £5.99 | |
| Beginners Thai | £5.99 | |
| Best Ever Slimmers' Recipes | £5.99 | |
| Best Food | £5.99 | |
| Best Food Desserts | £5.99 | |
| Best Food Mains | £5.99 | |
| Big Book of Beautiful Biscuits | £5.99 | |
| Biscuits & Slices | £5.99 | |
| Cakes & Slices Cookbook | £5.99 | |
| Cakes Cooking Class | £5.99 | |
| Caribbean Cooking | £5.99 | |
| Casseroles | £5.99 | |
| Celebration Cakes | £5.99 | |
| Chicken Meals in Minutes | £5.99 | |
| Chinese Cooking Class | £5.99 | |
| Christmas Book | £5.99 | |
| Christmas Cooking | £5.99 | |
| Cocktails | £5.99 | |
| Cooking for Crowds | £5.99 | |
| Cooking for Friends | £5.99 | |
| Cooking For Two | £5.99 | |
| Creative Cooking on a Budget | £5.99 | |
| Detox (Sept 05) | £5.99 | |
| Dinner Beef | £5.99 | |
| Dinner Lamb (Aug 05) | £5.99 | |
| Dinner Seafood | £5.99 | |
| Easy Australian Style | £5.99 | |
| Easy Curry | £5.99 | |
| Easy Spanish-Style | £5.99 | |
| Easy Vietnamese-Style | £5.99 | |
| Essential Barbecue | £5.99 | |
| Essential Microwave | £5.99 | |
| Essential Soup | £5.99 | |
| Freezer, Meals from the | £5.99 | |
| French Cooking Class | £5.99 | |

| TITLE | RRP | QTY |
|---|---|---|
| French Food, New | £5.99 | |
| Get Real, Make a Meal | £5.99 | |
| Good Food Fast | £5.99 | |
| Great Beef Cookbook | £5.99 | |
| Great Chicken Cookbook | £5.99 | |
| Great Lamb Cookbook | £5.99 | |
| Greek Cooking Class | £5.99 | |
| Healthy Heart Cookbook | £5.99 | |
| Indian Cooking Class | £5.99 | |
| Italian Cooking Class | £5.99 | |
| Japanese Cooking Class | £5.99 | |
| Kids' Birthday Cakes | £5.99 | |
| Kids Cooking | £5.99 | |
| Lean Food | £5.99 | |
| Low-fat Feasts | £5.99 | |
| Low-fat Food For Life | £5.99 | |
| Low-fat Meals in Minutes | £5.99 | |
| Main Course Salads | £5.99 | |
| Meals in Minutes | £5.99 | |
| Mediterranean Cookbook | £5.99 | |
| Middle Eastern Cooking Class | £5.99 | |
| Midweek Meals in Minutes | £5.99 | |
| Muffins, Scones & Bread | £5.99 | |
| New Finger Food | £5.99 | |
| Pasta Cookbook | £5.99 | |
| Pasta Meals in Minutes | £5.99 | |
| Potatoes | £5.99 | |
| Quick Meals in Minutes | £5.99 | |
| Quick-mix Biscuits & Slices | £5.99 | |
| Quick-mix Cakes | £5.99 | |
| Salads: Simple, Fast & Fresh | £5.99 | |
| Saucery | £5.99 | |
| Sensational Stir-Fries | £5.99 | |
| Short-order Cook | £5.99 | |
| Sweet Old Fashioned Favourites | £5.99 | |
| Thai Cooking Class | £5.99 | |
| Vegetarian Meals in Minutes | £5.99 | |
| Weekend Cook | £5.99 | |
| Wicked Sweet Indulgences | £5.99 | |
| Wok Meals in Minutes | £5.99 | |
| **TOTAL COST:** | £ | |

NAME

ADDRESS

POSTCODE

DAYTIME PHONE

I ENCLOSE MY CHEQUE/MONEY ORDER FOR £

OR PLEASE CHARGE MY VISA, ACCESS OR MASTERCARD NUMBER

CARD HOLDER'S NAME

EXPIRY DATE

CARDHOLDER'S SIGNATURE

**To order:** Mail or fax — photocopy or complete the order form above, and send your credit card details or cheque payable to: Australian Consolidated Press (UK), Moulton Park Business Centre, Red House Road, Moulton Park, Northampton NN3 6AQ, phone (+44) (0) 1604 497531, fax (+44) (0) 1604 497533, e-mail books@acpuk.com
**Non-UK residents:** We accept the credit cards listed on the coupon, or cheques, drafts or International Money Orders payable in sterling and drawn on a UK bank. Credit card charges are at the exchange rate current at the time of payment.
**Postage and packing:** Within the UK, add £1.50 for one book or £3.00 for two books. There is no postal charge for orders of three or more books for delivery within the UK. For delivery outside the UK, please phone, fax or e-mail for a quote.
**Offer ends 31.12.2005**

Test Kitchen
Food director *Pamela Clark*
Deputy food editor *Jan Castorina*
Assistant food editor *Kathy Snowball*
Associate food editor *Enid Morrison*
Senior home economists *Alexandra McGowan, Louise Patniotis, Kathy Wharton*
Home economists *Cynthia Black, Leisel Chen, Kathy McGarry, Tracey Port, Maggie Quickenden, Dimitra Stais*
Editorial coordinator *Elizabeth Hooper*
Kitchen assistant *Amy Wong*

ACP Books
Editorial director *Susan Tomnay*
Creative director *Hieu Chi Nguyen*
Editor *Stephanie Kistner*
Designer *Corey Butler*
Studio manager *Caryl Wiggins*
Editorial coordinator *Merryn Pearse*
Sales director *Brian Cearnes*
Publishing manager (rights & new projects) *Jane Hazell*
Marketing manager *Katie Graham*
Brand manager *Renée Crea*
Sales & marketing coordinator *Gabrielle Botto*
Pre-press *Harry Palmer*
Production manager *Carol Currie*
Business manager *Seymour Cohen*
Business analyst *Martin Howes*
Chief executive officer *John Alexander*
Group publisher *Pat Ingram*
Publisher *Sue Wannan*
Editor-in-chief *Deborah Thomas*

Produced by ACP Books, Sydney.
Printed by Times Printers, Singapore.
Published by ACP Publishing Pty Limited, 54 Park St, Sydney; GPO Box 4088, Sydney, NSW 2001.
Ph: (02) 9282 8618 Fax: (02) 9267 9438.
acpbooks@acp.com.au
www.acpbooks.com.au
To order books, phone 136 116.
Send recipe enquiries to:
recipeenquiries@acp.com.au

AUSTRALIA: Distributed by Network Services, GPO Box 4088, Sydney, NSW 2001.
Ph: (02) 9282 8777 Fax: (02) 9264 3278.
UNITED KINGDOM: Distributed by Australian Consolidated Press (UK), Moulton Park Business Centre, Red House Rd, Moulton Park, Northampton, NN3 6AQ.
Ph: (01604) 497531 Fax: (01604) 497533
acpukltd@aol.com
CANADA: Distributed by Whitecap Books Ltd, 351 Lynn Ave, North Vancouver, BC, V7J 2C4.
Ph: (604) 980 9852 Fax: (604) 980 8197
customerservice@whitecap.ca
www.whitecap.ca
NEW ZEALAND: Distributed by Netlink Distribution Company, ACP Media Centre, Cnr Fanshawe and Beaumont Streets, Westhaven, Auckland.
PO Box 47906, Ponsonby, Auckland, NZ.
Ph: (09) 366 9966 ask@ndcnz.co.nz
SOUTH AFRICA: Distributed by PSD Promotions 30 Diesel Road Isando, Gauteng, Johannesburg
PO Box 1175, Isando 1600, Gauteng, Johannesburg.
Ph: (2711) 392 6065 Fax: (2711) 392 6079
orders@psdprom.co.za

Clark, Pamela.
The Australian women's weekly cooking class Greek.
Rev ed.
Includes index.
ISBN 1 86396 461 4
1. Cookery, Greek. I. Title.
II. Title: Australian women's weekly.
641.59495


ABN 18 053 273 546

First published 1993. Reprinted 1993, 1997, 1999, 2000, 2001, 2002, 2004.
Revised and updated 2005.